# Workshop on Applied Textual Inference 2009

# (TextInfer 2009)



**Held at ACL-IJCNLP 2009**

## Singapore
## 6 August 2009

**ISBN: 978-1-61738-446-2**

**Printed from e-media with permission by:**

Curran Associates, Inc.
57 Morehouse Lane
Red Hook, NY 12571
www.proceedings.com

**Some format issues inherent in the e-media version may also appear in this print version.**



Printed by Curran Associates, Inc. (2010)



Association for Computational Linguistics
209 N. Eighth Street
Stroudsburg, Pennsylvania 18360

Phone: 1-570-476-8006
Fax: 1-570-476-0860

acl@aclweb.org

# Introduction

Applied textual inference has attracted a significant amount of attention in recent years. Recognizing textual entailments and detecting semantic equivalences between texts are at the core of many NLP tasks, including question answering, information extraction, text summarization, and many others. Developing generic algorithms and resources for inference and paraphrasing would therefore be applicable to a broad range of NLP applications.

The success of the first three Recognizing Textual Entailment (RTE) Pascal challenges and the high participation in this year's NIST-organized RTE challenge show that there is a very substantial interest in the area among the research community. RTE and paraphrase detection tasks have considerably stimulated research in the area of applied semantics, and computational models for textual inference are becoming more and more reliable and accurate as a result.

The goal of this workshop is to provide a common forum where people can discuss and compare novel ideas, models and tools for textual inference and paraphrasing. The workshop follows previous ACL workshops on these topics (the ACL workshop on "Empirical Modeling of Semantic Equivalence and Entailment", 2005, and the joint ACL-PASCAL workshop "Textual Entailment and Paraphrasing", 2007). This line of workshops goes in parallel with the RTE challenges, now organized by NIST, by promoting a deeper understanding of what are the scientific achievements and the new findings emerging in the field.

We would like to thank all the people that made this workshop possible: the people that submitted a paper, the reviewers, and the participants.

Enjoy the workshop!

The workshop organizers,

Chris Callison-Burch, John Hopkins Univesity (Program Co-chair)
Ido Dagan, Bar Ilan University
Christopher Manning, University of Stanford
Marco Pennacchiotti, Yahoo Research Labs
Fabio Massimo Zanzotto, University of Rome "Tor Vergata" (Program Co-chair)

**Organizers:**

Chris Callison-Burch, John Hopkins Univesity (Program Co-chair)
Ido Dagan, Bar Ilan University
Christopher Manning, University of Stanford
Marco Pennacchiotti, Yahoo Research Labs
Fabio Massimo Zanzotto, University of Rome "Tor Vergata" (Program Co-chair)

**Program Committee:**

Regina Barzilay, MIT
Johan Bos, University of Rome "La Sapienza"
Bill Dolan, Microsoft Research
Mark Dras, Macquarie University
Anette Frank, University of Heidelberg
Graeme Hirst, University of Toronto
Kentaro Inui, Nara Institute of Science and Technology
Bill MacCartney, Stanford University
Bernardo Magnini, FBK-irst
Katja Markert, University of Leeds
Rada Mihalcea, University of North Texas
Dan Moldovan, University of Texas at Dallas
Alessandro Moschitti, University of Trento
Kiyonori Ohtake, ATR
Sebastian Pado, University of Stanford
Manfred Pinkal, Saarland University
Dan Roth, University of Illinois at Urbana-Champaign
Satoshi Sato, Nagoya University
Satoshi Sekine, New York University
Idan Szpektor, Bar Ilan University
Stefan Thater, Saarland University
Kentaro Torisawa, NICT
Lucy Vanderwende, Microsoft Research
Annie Zaenen, PARC

# Table of Contents

# Conference Program

**Thursday, August 6, 2009**

8:45–9:00 Opening Remarks

**Session 1: Foundational Aspects and Linguistic Analysis of Textual Entailment**

9:00–9:30 *Multi-word expressions in textual inference: Much ado about nothing?*
Marie-Catherine de Marneffe, Sebastian Pado and Christopher D. Manning

9:30–10:00 *A Proposal on Evaluation Measures for RTE*
Richard Bergmair

10:00–10:30 Coffee Break

10:30–11:00 *Sub-sentencial Paraphrasing by Contextual Pivot Translation*
Aurélien Max

11:00–12:00 Invited Talks

12:00–13.50 Lunch

**Session 2: Learning Textual Entailment Rules and Building Corpora**

13:50–14:20 *Augmenting WordNet-based Inference with Argument Mapping*
Idan Szpektor and Ido Dagan

14:20–14:50 *Optimizing Textual Entailment Recognition Using Particle Swarm Optimization*
Yashar Mehdad and Bernardo Magnini

14:50–15.10 *Ranking Paraphrases in Context*
Stefan Thater, Georgiana Dinu and Manfred Pinkal

15:10–15:30 *Building an Annotated Textual Inference Corpus for Motion and Space*
Kirk Roberts

15:30–16:00 Coffee Break

**Thursday, August 6, 2009 (continued)**

**Session 3: Machine Learning Models and Application of Textual Inference**

16:00–16:30 *Using Hypernymy Acquisition to Tackle (Part of) Textual Entailment*
Elena Akhmatova and Mark Dras

16:30–17:00 *Automating Model Building in c-rater*
Jana Sukkarieh and Svetlana Stoyanchev

17:00–17:20 *Presupposed Content and Entailments in Natural Language Inference*
David Clausen and Christopher D. Manning

17:20–18:00 Final Panel and Discussion

# Multi-word expressions in textual inference: Much ado about nothing?

**Marie-Catherine de Marneffe**
Linguistics Department
Stanford University
Stanford, CA
mcdm@stanford.edu

**Sebastian Padó**
Institut für Maschinelle Sprachverarbeitung
Stuttgart University, Germany
pado@ims.uni-stuttgart.de

**Christopher D. Manning**
Computer Science Department
Stanford University
Stanford, CA
manning@stanford.edu

## Abstract

Multi-word expressions (MWE) have seen much attention from the NLP community. In this paper, we investigate their impact on the recognition of textual entailment (RTE). Using the manual Microsoft Research annotations, we first manually count and classify MWEs in RTE data. We find few, most of which are arguably unlikely to cause processing problems. We then consider the impact of MWEs on a current RTE system. We are unable to confirm that entailment recognition suffers from wrongly aligned MWEs. In addition, MWE alignment is difficult to improve, since MWEs are poorly represented in state-of-the-art paraphrase resources, the only available sources for multi-word similarities. We conclude that RTE should concentrate on other phenomena impacting entailment, and that paraphrase knowledge is best understood as capturing general lexico-syntactic variation.

## 1 Introduction

*Multi-word expressions* (MWEs) can be defined as "idiosyncratic interpretations that cross word boundaries", such as *traffic light* or *kick the bucket*. Called a "pain in the neck for NLP", they have received considerable attention in recent years and it has been suggested that proper treatment could make a significant difference in various NLP tasks (Sag et al., 2002). The importance attributed to them is also reflected in a number of workshops (Bond et al., 2003; Tanaka et al., 2004; Moirón et al., 2006; Grégoire et al., 2007). However, there are few detailed breakdowns of the benefits that improved MWE handling provides to applications.

This paper investigates the impact of MWEs on the "recognition of textual entailment" (RTE) task (Dagan et al., 2006). Our analysis ties in with the pivotal question of what types of knowledge are beneficial for RTE. A number of papers have suggested that *paraphrase knowledge* plays a very important role (Bar-Haim et al., 2005; Marsi et al., 2007; Dinu and Wang, 2009). For example, Bar-Haim et al. (2005) conclude: "Our analysis also shows that paraphrases stand out as a dominant contributor to the entailment task."

The term "paraphrase" is however often construed broadly. In Bar-Haim et al. (2005), it refers to the ability of relating *lexico-syntactic* reformulations such as diathesis alternations, passivizations, or symmetrical predicates (*X lent his BMW to Y*/*Y borrowed X's BMW*). If "paraphrase" simply refers to the use of a language's lexical and syntactic possibilities to express equivalent meaning in different ways, then paraphrases are certainly important to RTE. But such a claim means little more than that RTE can profit from good understanding of syntax and semantics. However, given the abovementioned interest in MWEs, there is another possibility: does success in RTE involve proper handling of MWEs, such as knowing that *take a pass on* is equivalent to *aren't purchasing*, or *kicked the bucket* to *died*? This seems not too far-fetched: Knowledge about MWEs is under-represented in existing semantic resources like WordNet or distributional thesauri, but should be present in paraphrase resources, which provide similarity judgments between phrase pairs, including MWEs.

The goal of our study is to investigate the merits of this second, more precise, hypothesis, measuring the impact of MWE processing on RTE. In the absence of a universally accepted definition of MWEs, we define MWEs in the RTE setting as *multi-word alignments*, i.e., words that participate in more than one word alignment link between premise and hypothesis:

(1)
PRE: He died.
HYP: He kicked the bucket.

The exclusion of MWEs that do not lead to multi-word alignments (i.e., which can be aligned word by word) is not a significant loss, since these cases are unlikely to cause significant problems for RTE. In addition, an alignment-based approach has the advantage of generality: Almost all existing RTE models *align* the linguistic material of the premise



*Proceedings of the 2009 Workshop on Applied Textual Inference, ACL-IJCNLP 2009*, pages 1–9,
Suntec, Singapore, 6 August 2009. 

and hypothesis and base at least part of their decision on properties of this alignment (Burchardt et al., 2007; Hickl and Bensley, 2007; Iftene and Balahur-Dobrescu, 2007; Zanzotto et al., 2007).

We proceed in three steps. First, we analyze the Microsoft Research (MSR) manual word alignments (Brockett, 2007) for the RTE2 dataset (Bar-Haim et al., 2006), shedding light on the relationship between alignments and multi-word expressions. We provide frequency estimates and a coarse-grained classification scheme for multi-word expressions on textual entailment data. Next, we analyze two widely used types of paraphrase resources with respect to their modeling of MWEs. Finally, we investigate the impact of MWEs and their handling on practical entailment recognition.

## 2 Multi-Word Expressions in Alignment

Almost all textual entailment recognition models incorporate an alignment procedure that establishes correspondences between the premise and the hypothesis. The computation of word alignments is usually phrased as an optimization task. The search space is based on lexical similarities, but usually extended with *structural biases* in order to obtain alignments with desirable properties, such as the contiguous alignment of adjacent words, or the mapping of different source words on to different target words. One prominent constraint of the IBM word alignment models (Brown et al., 1993) is *functional alignment*, that is each target word is mapped onto *at most* one source word. Other models produce only *one-to-one alignments*, where both alignment directions must be functional.

MWEs that involve many-to-many or one-to-many alignments like Ex. (1) present a problem for such constrained word alignment models. A functional alignment model can still handle cases like Ex. (1) correctly in one direction (from bottom to top), but not in the other one. One-to-one alignments manage neither. Various workarounds have been proposed in the MT literature, such as computing word alignments in both directions and forming the union or intersection. Even if an alignment is technically within the search space, accurate knowledge about plausible phrasal matches is necessary for it to be assigned a high score and thus identified.

## 3 MWEs in the RTE2 Dataset

In the first part of our study, we estimate the extent to which the inability of aligners to model one-to-many and many-to-many correspondences is an issue. To do so, we use the Microsoft Research manual alignments for the RTE2 data. To date, the MSR data constitutes the only gold standard alignment corpus publicly available. Since annotators were not constrained to use one-to-one alignments, we assume that the MSR alignments contain multi-word alignments where appropriate.

| | | CARDINALITY | |
|---|---|---|---|
| | | M-to-M | 1-to-M |
| DECOM- | yes | (1) | (3) |
| POSABLE? | no | (2) | (4) |
| OTHER | | | (5), (6), (7) |

Table 1: MWEs categories and definition criteria (M-to-M: many-to-many; 1-to-M: one-to-many).

From the MSR data, we extract all multi-word alignments that fall outside the scope of "functional" alignments, i.e., alignments of the form "many-to-many" or "one-to-many" (in the direction hypothesis-premise). We annotate them according to the categories defined below. The MSR data distinguishes between SURE and POSSIBLE alignments. We only take the SURE alignments into account. While this might mean missing some multi-word alignments, we found many "possible" links to be motivated by the desire to obtain a high-coverage alignment, as Ex. 2 shows:

(2)
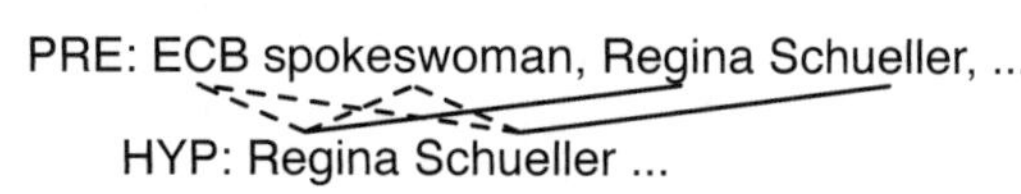


Here, the hypothesis words "Regina Schueller" are individually "sure"-aligned to the premise words "Regina Schueller" (solid lines), but are also both "possible"-linked to "ECB spokeswoman" (dashed lines). This "possible" alignment can be motivated on syntactic or referential grounds, but does not indicate a correspondence in meaning (as opposed to reference).

### 3.1 Analysis of Multi-Word Expressions

Table 1 shows the seven categories we define to distinguish the different types of multi-word alignments. We use two main complementary criteria for our annotation. The first one is the cardinality of the alignment: does it involve phrases proper on both sides (many-to-many), or just on one side (one-to-many)? The second one is decomposability: is it possible to create one or more one-to-one alignments that capture the main semantic contribution of the multi-word alignment? Our motivation for introducing this criterion is that even aligners that are unable to recover the complete MWE have a chance to identify the links crucial for entailment if the MWE is decomposable (categories (1) and (3)). This is not possible for the more difficult non-decomposable categories (2) and (4). The remaining categories, (5) to (7), involve auxiliaries, multiple mentions, and named entities, which are not MWEs in the narrow sense. We will henceforth use the term "true MWEs" to refer to categories (1)–(4), as opposed to (5)–(7).

The criteria we use for MWE categorization are different from the ones adopted by Sag et al. (2002). Sag et al.'s goal is to classify constructions by their range of admissible variation, and thus relies heavily on syntactic variability. Since we are more interested in semantic properties, we base our classes on alignment patterns, complemented by semantic decomposability judgments (which reflect the severity of treating MWEs like compositional phrases). As mentioned in Section 1, our method misses MWEs aligned with one-to-one links; however, the use of a one-to-one link by the annotation can be seen as evidence for decomposability.

**A. Multiple words on both sides**

(1) **Compositional phrases (CP)**:
Each word in the left phrase can be aligned to one word in the right phrase, e.g., *capital punishment* → *death penalty* for which *capital* can be aligned to *death* and *punishment* to *penalty*.

(2) **Non-compositional phrases (NCP)**:
There is no simple way to align words between the two phrases, such as in *poorly represented* → *very few* or *illegally entered* → *broke into*.

**B. One word to multiple words**

(3) **Headed multi-word expressions (MWEH)**:
A single word can be aligned with one token of an MWE: e.g., *vote* → *cast ballots* where *ballots* carries enough of the semantics of *vote*.

(4) **Non-headed MWEs (MWENH)**:
The MWE as a whole is necessary to capture the meaning of the single word, which doesn't align well to any individual word of the MWE: e.g., *ferry* → *passenger vessel*.

(5) **Multiple mentions (MENTION)**:
These alignments link one word to multiple occurrences of the same or related word(s) in the text, e.g., *military* → *forces ... Marines*, *antibiotics* → *antibiotics ... drug*.

(6) **Parts of named entities (PART)**:
Each element of a named entity is aligned to the whole named entity: e.g., *Shukla* → *Nidhi Shukla*. This includes the use of acronyms or abbreviations on one side and their spelled-out forms on the other side, such as *U.S.* → *United States*.

(7) **Auxiliaries (AUX)**:
The last category involves the presence of an auxiliary: e.g., *were* → *are being*.

| Status | Category | RTE2 dev | RTE2 test |
|---|---|---|---|
| decomp. | CP | 5 | 0 |
| | MWEH | 40 | 31 |
| non-decomp. | NCP | 6 | 0 |
| | MWENH | 30 | 29 |
| **Subtotal: True MWEs** | | **81** | **60** |
| other | MENTION | 26 | 48 |
| | PART | 82 | 54 |
| | AUX | 0 | 2 |
| **Total: All MWEs** | | 189 | 164 |

Table 2: Frequencies of sentences with different multi-word alignment categories in MSR data.

Initially, one of the authors used these categories to analyze the complete RTE2 MSR data (dev and test sets). The most difficult distinction to draw was, not surprisingly, the decision between decomposable multi-word alignments (categories (1) and (3)) and non-decomposable ones (categories (2) and (4)). To ascertain that a reliable distinction can be made, another author did an independent second analysis of the instances from categories (1) through (4). We found moderate inter-annotator agreement ($\kappa$ = 0.60), indicating that not all, but most annotation decisions are uncontroversial.

### 3.2 Distribution of Multi-Word Expressions

Table 2 shows the distribution in the MSR data of all alignment categories. Our evaluation will concentrate on the "true MWE" categories (1) to (4): CP, NCP, MWEH and MWENH.[1]

[1]The OTHER categories (5) to (7) can generally be dealt with during pre- or post-processing: Auxiliary-verb combinations (cat. 7) are usually "headed" so that it is sufficient to align the main verb; multiple occurrences of words referring to the same entity (cat. 5) is an anaphor resolution problem; and named-entity matches (cat. 6) are best solved by using a named entity recognizer to collapse NEs into a single token.

In RTE2 dev and test, we find only 81 and 60 true MWEs, respectively. Out of the 1600 sentence pairs in the two datasets, 8.2% involve true MWEs (73 in RTE2 dev and 58 in RTE2 test). On the level of word alignments, the ratio is even smaller: only 1.2% of all SURE alignments involve true MWEs. Furthermore, more than half of them are decomposable (MWEH/CP). Some examples from this category are ("heads" marked in boldface):

*sue*→ *file* ***lawsuits*** *against*
*diseases* → *liver* ***cancer***
*Barbie* → ***Barbie*** *doll*
*got* → *was* ***awarded*** *with*
*works* → *executive* ***director***
*military* → *naval* ***forces***

In particular when light verbs are involved (*file lawsuits*) or when modification adds just minor meaning aspects (*executive director*), we argue that it is sufficient to align the left-hand expression to the "head" in order to decide entailment.

Consider, in contrast, these examples from the non-decomposable categories (MWENH/NCP):

*politician* → *presidential candidate*
*killed* → *lost their lives*
*shipwreck* → *sunken ship*
*ever* → *in its history*
*widow* → *late husband*
*sexes* → *men and women*

These cases span a broad range of linguistic relations from pure associations (*widow/late husband*) to collective expressions (*sexes/men and women*). Arguably, in these cases aligning the left-hand word to any single word on the right can seriously throw off an entailment recognition system. However, they are fairly rare, occurring only in 65 out of 1600 sentences.

### 3.3 Conclusions from the MSR Analysis

Our analysis has found that 8% of the sentences in the MSR dataset involve true MWEs. At the word level, the fraction of true MWEs of all SURE alignment links is just over 1%.

Of course, if errors in the alignment of these MWEs had a high probability to lead to entailment recognition errors, MWEs would still constitute a major factor in determining entailment. However, we have argued that about half of the true MWEs are *decomposable*, that is, the part of the alignment that is crucial for entailment can be recovered with a one-to-one alignment link that can be identified even by very limited alignment models.

This leaves considerably less than 1% of all word alignments (or ∼4% of sentence pairs) where imperfect MWE alignments *are able at all* to exert a negative influence on entailment. However, this is just an upper bound – their impact is by no means guaranteed. Thus, our conclusion from the annotation study is that we do not expect MWEs to play a large role in actual entailment recognition.

## 4 MWEs in Paraphrase Resources

Before we come to actual experiments on the automatic recognition of MWEs in a practical RTE system, we need to consider the prerequisites for this task. As mentioned in Section 2, if an RTE system is to establish multi-word alignments, it requires a knowledge source that provides accurate semantic similarity judgments for "many-to-many" alignments (*capital punishment* – *death penalty*) as well as for "one-to-many" alignments (*vote* – *cast ballots*). Such similarities are not present in standard lexical resources like WordNet or Dekang Lin's thesaurus (Lin, 1998).

The best class of candidate resources to provide wide-coverage of multi-word similarities seems to be *paraphrase* resources. In this section, we examine to what extent two of the most widely used paraphrase resource types provide supporting evidence for the true MWEs in the MSR data. We deliberately use corpus-derived, noisy resources, since we are interested in the real-world (rather than idealized) prospects for accurate MWE alignment.

**Dependency-based paraphrases.** Lin and Pantel (2002)'s DIRT model collects lexicalized dependency paths with two slots at either end. Paths with similar distributions over slot fillers count as paraphrases, with the quality measured by a mutual information-based similarity over the slot fillers. The outcome of their study is the DIRT database which lists paraphrases for around 230,000 dependency paths, extracted from about 1 GB of miscellaneous newswire text. We converted the DIRT paraphrases[2] into a resource of semantic similarities between raw text phrases. We used a heuristic mapping from dependency relations to word order, and obtained similarity ratings by rescaling the DIRT paraphrase ratings, which are based on a mutual information-based measure of filler similarity, onto the range [0,1].

[2]We thank Patrick Pantel for granting us access to DIRT.

**Parallel corpora-based paraphrases.** An alternative approach to paraphrase acquisition was proposed by Bannard and Callison-Burch (2005). It exploits the variance inherent in translation to extract paraphrases from bilingual parallel corpora. Concretely, it observes translational relationships between a source and a target language and pairs up source language phrases with other source language phrases that translate into the same target language phrases. We applied this method to the large Chinese-English GALE MT evaluation P3/P3.5 corpus ($\sim$2 GB text per language, mostly newswire). The large number of translations makes it impractical to store all observed paraphrases. We therefore filtered the list of paraphrases against the raw text of the RTE corpora, acquiring the 10 best paraphrases for around 100,000 two- and three-word phrases. The MLE conditional probabilities were scaled onto [0,1] for each target.

**Analysis.** We checked the two resources for the presence of the true MWEs identified in the MSR data. We found that overall 34% of the MWEs appear in these resources, with more decomposable MWEs (MWEH/CP) than non-decomposable ones (MWENH/NCP) (42.1% vs. 24.6%). However, we find that almost all of the MWEs that are covered by the paraphrase resources are assigned very low scores, while erroneous paraphrases (expressions with clearly different meanings) have higher scores. This is illustrated in Table 3 for the case of *poorly represented*, which is aligned to *very few* in one RTE2 sentence. This paraphrase is on the list, but with a lower similarity than unsuitable paraphrases such as *representatives* or *good*. This problem is widespread. Other examples of low-scoring paraphrases are: *another step* → *measures*, *quarantine* → *in isolation*, *punitive measures* → *sanctions*, *held a position* → *served as*, or *inability* → *could not*.

The noise in the rankings means that any alignment algorithm faces a dilemma: either it uses a high threshold and misses valid MWE alignments, or it lowers its threshold and risks constructing incorrect alignments.

## 5 Impact of MWEs on Practical Entailment Recognition

This section provides the final step in our study: an evaluation of the impact of MWEs on entailment recognition in a current RTE system, and of the benefits of explicit MWE alignment. While the

| **poorly represented** | |
|---|---|
| represented | 0.42 |
| poorly | 0.07 |
| rarely | 0.06 |
| good | 0.05 |
| representatives | 0.04 |
| very few | 0.04 |
| well | 0.02 |
| representative | 0.01 |

Table 3: Paraphrases of "poorly represented" with scores (semantic similarities).

results of this experiment are not guaranteed to transfer to other RTE system architectures, or to future, improved paraphrase resources, it provides a current snapshot of the practical impact of MWE handling.

### 5.1 The Stanford RTE System

We base our experiments on the Stanford RTE system which uses a staged architecture (MacCartney et al., 2006). After the linguistic analysis which produces dependency graphs for premise and hypothesis, the alignment stage creates links between the nodes of the two dependency trees. In the inference stage, the system produces roughly 70 features for the aligned premise-hypothesis pair, almost all of which are implementations of "small linguistic theories" whose activation indicates lexical, syntactic and semantic matches and mismatches of different types. The entailment decision is computed using a logistic regression on these features.

The Stanford system supports the use of different aligners without touching the rest of the pipeline. We compare two aligners: a one-to-one aligner, which cannot construct MWE alignments (UNIQ), and a many-to-many aligner (MANLI) (MacCartney et al., 2008), which can. Both aligners use around 10 large-coverage lexical resources of semantic similarities, both manually compiled resources (such as WordNet and NomBank) and automatically induced resources (such as Dekang Lin's distributional thesaurus or InfoMap).

**UNIQ: A one-to-one aligner.** UNIQ constructs an alignment between dependency graphs as the highest-scoring mapping from each word in the hypothesis to one word in the premise, or to null. Mappings are scored by summing the alignment scores of all individual word pairs (provided by the lexical resources), plus edge alignment scores that use the syntactic structure of premise and hypothesis to introduce a bias for syntactic parallelism. The large number of possible alignments (exponential in the number of hypothesis words) makes exhaustive search intractable. Instead, UNIQ uses a stochastic search based on Gibbs sampling, a well-known Markov Chain Monte Carlo technique (see de Marneffe et al. (2007) for details).

Since it does not support many-to-many alignments, the UNIQ aligner cannot make use of the multi-word information present in the paraphrase resources. To be able to capture some common MWEs, the Stanford RTE system was originally designed with a facility to concatenate MWEs present in WordNet into a single token (mostly particle verbs and collocations, e.g., *treat_as* or *foreign_minister*). However, we discovered that WordNet collapsing always has a negative effect. Inspection of the constructed alignments suggests that the lexical resources that inform the alignment process do not provide scores for most collapsed tokens (such as *wait_for*), and precision suffers.

**MANLI: A phrase-to-phrase aligner.** MANLI aims at finding an optimal alignment between phrases, defined as contiguous spans of one or multiple words. MANLI characterizes alignments as *edit scripts*, sets of edits (substitutions, deletions, and insertions) over phrases. The quality of an edit script is the sum of the quality of the individual edit steps. Individual edits are scored using a feature-based scoring function that takes edit type and size into consideration.[3] The score for substitution edits also includes a lexical similarity score similar to UNIQ, plus potential knowledge about the semantic relatedness of multi-word phrases not expressible in UNIQ. Substitution edits also use contextual features, including a distortion score and a matching-neighbors feature.[4] Due to the dependence between alignment and segmentation decisions, MANLI uses a simulated annealing strategy to traverse the resulting large search space.

Even though MANLI is our current best candidate at recovering MWE alignments, it currently has an important architectural limitation: it works on textual phrases rather than dependency tree fragments, and therefore misses all MWEs that are not contiguous (e.g., due to inserted articles or adverbials). This accounts for roughly 9% of the MWEs in RTE2 data. Other work on RTE has targeted specifically this observation and has described paraphrases on a dependency level (Marsi et al., 2007; Dinu and Wang, 2009).

| | | micro-avg | | |
|---|---|---|---|---|
| | | P | R | $F_1$ |
| UNIQ | w/o para | 80.4 | 80.8 | 80.6 |
| MANLI | w/o para | 77.0 | 85.5 | 81.0 |
| | w/ para | 76.7 | 85.4 | 80.8 |

Table 4: Evaluation of aligners and resources against the manual MSR RTE2 test annotations.

**Setup.** To set the parameters of the two models (i.e., the weights for different lexical resources for UNIQ, and the weights for the edit operation for MANLI), we use the RTE2 development data. Testing takes place on the RTE2 test and RTE4 datasets. For MANLI, we performed this procedure twice, with the paraphrase resources described in Section 4 once deactivated and once activated. We evaluated the output of the Stanford RTE system both on the word alignment level, and on the entailment decision level.

### 5.2 Evaluation of Alignment Accuracy

The results for evaluating the MANLI and UNIQ alignments against the manual alignment links in the MSR RTE2 test set are given in Table 4. We present micro-averaged numbers, where each alignment link counts equally (i.e., longer problems have a larger impact). The overall difference is not large, but MANLI produces a slightly better alignment.

The ability of MANLI to construct many-to-many alignments is reflected in a different position on the precision/recall curve: the MANLI aligner is less precise than UNIQ, but has a higher recall. Examples for UNIQ and MANLI alignments are shown in Figures 1 and 2. A comparison of the alignments shows the pattern to be expected from Table 4: MANLI has a higher recall, but contains occasional questionable links, such as *at President* $\rightarrow$ *President* in Figure 1.

However, the many-to-many alignments that MANLI produces do not correspond well to the MWE alignments. The overall impact of the paraphrase resources is very small, and their addition actually hurts MANLI's performance slightly. A more detailed analysis revealed two contrary trends. On the one hand, the paraphrase resources provide

[3]Positive weights for all operation types ensure that MANLI prefers small over large edits where appropriate.

[4]An adaptation of the averaged perceptron algorithm (Collins, 2002) is used to tune the model parameters.

| Aligner | w/o para | w/ para |
|---|---|---|
| UNIQ | 63.8 | – |
| MANLI | 60.6 | 60.6 |

Table 5: Entailment recognition accuracy of the Stanford system on RTE2 test (two-way task).

| Aligner | w/o para | w/ para | TAC system |
|---|---|---|---|
| UNIQ | 63.3 | – | 61.4 |
| MANLI | 59.0 | 57.9 | 57.0 |

Table 6: Entailment recognition accuracy of the Stanford system on RTE4 (two-way task).

beneficial information, maybe surprisingly, in the form of broad distributional similarities for *single* words that were not available from the standard lexical resources (e.g., the alignment "the company's *letter*" → "the company's *certificate*").

On the other hand, MANLI captures not one of the true MWEs identified in the MSR data. It only finds two many-to-many alignments which belong to the CP category: *aimed criticism* → *has criticised, European currency* → *euro currency*. We see this as the practical consequences of our observation from Section 4: The scores in current paraphrase resources are too noisy to support accurate MWE recognition (cf. Table 3).

### 5.3 Evaluation of Entailment Recognition

We finally evaluated the performance of the Stanford system using UNIQ and MANLI alignments on the entailment task. We consider two datasets: RTE2 test, the alignment evaluation dataset, and the most recent RTE4 dataset, where current numbers for the Stanford system are available from last year's Text Analysis Conference (TAC).

A reasonable conjecture would be that better alignments translate into better entailment recognition. However, as the results in Tables 5 and 6 show, this is not the case. Overall, UNIQ outperforms MANLI by several percent accuracy despite MANLI's better alignments. This "baseline" difference should not be overinterpreted, since it may be setup-specific: the features computed in the inference stage of the Stanford system were developed mainly with the UNIQ aligner in mind. A more significant result is that the integration of paraphrase knowledge in MANLI has no effect on RTE2 test, and even decreases performance on RTE4.

The general picture that we observe is that there is only a loose coupling between alignments and the entailment decision: individual alignments seldom matter. This is shown, for example, by the alignments in Figures 1 and 2. Even though MANLI provides a better overall alignment, UNIQ's alignment is "good enough" for entailment purposes. In Figure 1, the two words UNIQ leaves unaligned are a preposition (*at*) and a light verb (*aimed*), both of which are not critical to determine whether or not the premise entails the hypothesis.

This interpretation is supported by another analysis, where we tested whether entailments involving at least one true MWE are more difficult to recognize. We computed the entailment accuracy for all applicable RTE2 test pairs (7%, 58 sentences). The accuracy on this subset is 62% for the MANLI model without paraphrases, 64% for the MANLI model with paraphrases, and 74% for UNIQ. The differences from the numbers in Table 5 are not significant due to the small size of the MWE sample, but we observe that the accuracy on the MWE subset tends to be *higher* than on the whole set (rather than lower). Futhermore, even though we finally see a small beneficial effect of paraphrases on the MANLI aligner, the UNIQ aligner, which completely ignores MWEs, still performs substantially better.

Our conclusion is that wrong entailment decisions rarely hinge on wrongly aligned MWEs, at least with a probabilistic architecture like the Stanford system. Consequently, it suffices to recover the most crucial alignment links to predict entailment, and the benefits associated with the use of a more *restricted* alignment formulation, like the one-to-one alignment formulation of UNIQ, outweighs those of more powerful alignment models, like MANLI's phrasal alignments.

## 6 Conclusions

We have investigated the influence of multi-word expressions on the task of recognizing textual entailment. In contrast to the widely held view that proper treatment of MWEs could bring about a substantial improvement in NLP tasks, we found that the importance of MWEs in RTE is rather small. Among the MWEs that we identified in the alignments, more than half can be captured by one-to-one alignments, and should not pose problems for entailment recognition.

Furthermore, we found that the remaining MWEs are rather difficult to model faithfully. The MSR MWEs are poorly represented in state-of-the-

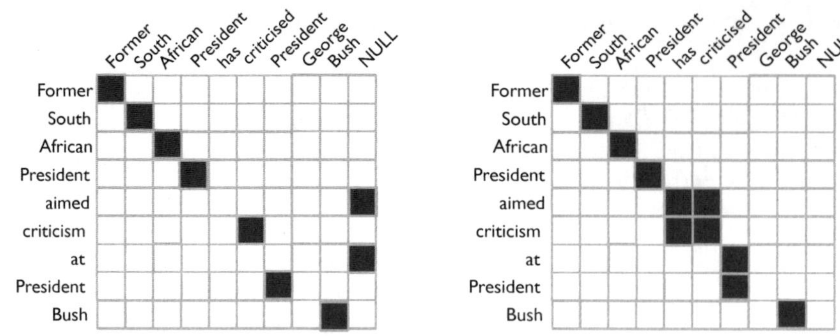


Figure 1: UNIQ (left) and MANLI (right) alignments for problem 483 in RTE2 test. The rows represent the hypothesis words, and the columns the premise words.

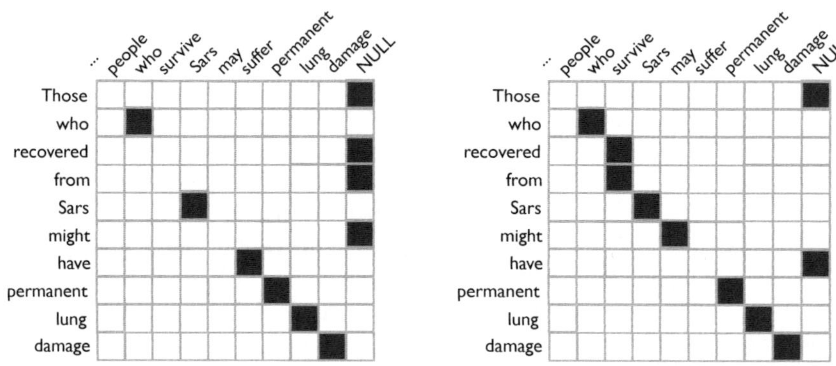


Figure 2: UNIQ (left) and MANLI (right) alignments for problem 1 in RTE2 test.

art lexical resources, and when they are present, scoring issues arise. Consequently, at least in the Stanford system, the integration of paraphrase knowledge to enable MWE recognition has made almost no difference either in terms of alignment accuracy nor in entailment accuracy. Furthermore, it is not the case that entailment recognition accuracy is worse for sentences with "true" MWEs. In sum, we find that even though capturing and representing MWEs is an interesting problem in itself, MWEs do not seem to be such a pain in the neck – at least not for textual entailment.

Our results may seem to contradict the results of many previous RTE studies such as (Bar-Haim et al., 2005) which found paraphrases to make an important contribution. However, the beneficial effect of paraphrases found in these studies refers not to an alignment task, but to the ability of relating *lexico-syntactic* reformulations such as diathesis alternations or symmetrical predicates (*buy/sell*). In the Stanford system, this kind of knowledge is already present in the features of the inference stage. Our results should therefore rather be seen as a clarification of the complementary nature of the paraphrase and MWE issues.

In our opinion, there is much more potential for improvement from better estimates of semantic similarity. This is true for phrasal similarity, as our negative results for multi-word paraphrases show, but also on the single-word level. The 2% gain in accuracy for the Stanford system here over the reported TAC RTE4 results stems merely from efforts to clean up and rescale the lexical resources used by the system, and outweighs the effect of MWEs. One possible direction of research is conditioning semantic similarity on *context*: Most current lexical resources characterize similarity at the lemma level, but true similarities of word or phrase pairs are strongly context-dependent: *obtain* and *be awarded* are much better matches in the context of *a degree* than in the context of *data*.

## Acknowledgments

We thank Bill MacCartney for his help with the MANLI aligner, and Michel Galley for the parallel corpus-based paraphrase resource. This paper is based on work funded in part by DARPA through IBM. The content does not necessarily reflect the views of the U.S. Government, and no official endorsement should be inferred.

## References


Colin Bannard and Chris Callison-Burch. 2005. Paraphrasing with bilingual parallel corpora. In *Proceedings of the 43rd Annual Meeting of the Association for Computational Linguistics*, pages 597–604, Ann Arbor, MI.

Roy Bar-Haim, Idan Szpecktor, and Oren Glickman. 2005. Definition and analysis of intermediate entailment levels. In *Proceedings of the ACL Workshop on Empirical Modeling of Semantic Equivalence and Entailment*, pages 55–60, Ann Arbor, MI.

Roy Bar-Haim, Ido Dagan, Bill Dolan, Lisa Ferro, Danilo Giampiccolo, Bernardo Magnini, and Idan Szpektor. 2006. The second PASCAL recognising textual entailment challenge. In *Proceedings of the Second PASCAL Challenges Workshop on Recognising Textual Entailment*, Venice, Italy.

Francis Bond, Anna Korhonen, Diana McCarthy, and Aline Villavicencio, editors. 2003. *Proceedings of the ACL 2003 workshop on multiword expressions: Analysis, acquisition and treatment.*

Chris Brockett. 2007. Aligning the RTE 2006 corpus. Technical Report MSR-TR-2007-77, Microsoft Research.

Peter F. Brown, Stephen Della Pietra, Vincent J. Della Pietra, and Robert L. Mercer. 1993. The mathematic of statistical machine translation: Parameter estimation. *Computational Linguistics*, 19(2):263–311.

Aljoscha Burchardt, Nils Reiter, Stefan Thater, and Anette Frank. 2007. A semantic approach to textual entailment: System evaluation and task analysis. In *Proceedings of the ACL-PASCAL Workshop on Textual Entailment and Paraphrasing*, pages 10–15, Prague, Czech Republic.

Michael Collins. 2002. Discriminative training methods for hidden Markov models. In *Proceedings of the Conference on Empirical Methods in Natural Language Processing*.

Ido Dagan, Oren Glickman, and Bernardo Magnini. 2006. The PASCAL recognising textual entailment challenge. In J. Quinonero-Candela, I. Dagan, B. Magnini, and F. d'Alch Buc, editors, *Machine Learning Challenges. Lecture Notes in Computer Science, Vol. 3944*, pages 177–190. Springer.

Marie-Catherine de Marneffe, Trond Grenager, Bill MacCartney, Daniel Cer, Daniel Ramage, Chloé Kiddon, and Christopher D. Manning. 2007. Aligning semantic graphs for textual inference and machine reading. In *Proceedings of the AAAI Spring Symposium*.

Georgiana Dinu and Rui Wang. 2009. Inference rules and their application to recognizing textual entailment. In *Proceedings of the 12th Conference of the European Chapter of the ACL (EACL 2009)*, pages 211–219, Athens, Greece.

Nicole Grégoire, Stefan Evert, and Su Nam Kim, editors. 2007. *Proceedings of the ACL workshop: A broader perspective on multiword expressions.*

Andrew Hickl and Jeremy Bensley. 2007. A discourse commitment-based framework for recognizing textual entailment. In *Proceedings of the ACL-PASCAL Workshop on Textual Entailment and Paraphrasing*, pages 171–176, Prague, Czech Republic.

Adrian Iftene and Alexandra Balahur-Dobrescu. 2007. Hypothesis transformation and semantic variability rules used in recognizing textual entailment. In *Proceedings of the ACL-PASCAL Workshop on Textual Entailment and Paraphrasing*, pages 125–130, Prague, Czech Republic.

Dekang Lin and Patrick Pantel. 2002. Discovery of inference rules for question answering. *Journal of Natural Language Engineering*, 7(4):343–360.

Dekang Lin. 1998. Automatic retrieval and clustering of similar words. In *Proceedings of the joint Annual Meeting of the Association for Computational Linguistics and International Conference on Computational Linguistics*, pages 768–774, Montréal, Canada.

Bill MacCartney, Trond Grenager, Marie-Catherine de Marneffe, Daniel Cer, and Christopher D. Manning. 2006. Learning to recognize features of valid textual entailments. In *Proceedings of NAACL.*

Bill MacCartney, Michel Galley, and Christopher D. Manning. 2008. A phrase-based alignment model for natural language inference. In *Proceedings of the Conference on Empirical Methods in Natural Language Processing*, Honolulu, Hawaii.

Erwin Marsi, Emiel Krahmer, and Wauter Bosma. 2007. Dependency-based paraphrasing for recognizing textual entailment. In *Proceedings of the ACL-PASCAL Workshop on Textual Entailment and Paraphrasing*, pages 83–88, Prague, Czech Republic.

Begona Villada Moirón, Aline Villavicencio, Diana McCarthy, Stefan Evert, and Suzanne Stevenson, editors. 2006. *Proceedings of the ACL Workshop on Multiword Expressions: Identifying and Exploiting Underlying Properties.*

Ivan A. Sag, Timothy Baldwin, Francis Bond, Ann Copestake, and Dan Flickinger. 2002. Multi-word expressions: a pain in the neck for NLP. In *Proceedings of CICLing.*

Takaaki Tanaka, Aline Villavicencio, Francis Bond, and Anna Korhonen, editors. 2004. *Proceedings of the second ACL workshop on multiword expressions: Integrating processing.*

Fabio Massimo Zanzotto, Marco Pennacchiotti, and Alessandro Moschitti. 2007. Shallow semantic in fast textual entailment rule learners. In *Proceedings of the ACL-PASCAL Workshop on Textual Entailment and Paraphrasing*, pages 72–77, Prague, Czech Republic.

# A Proposal on Evaluation Measures for RTE

**Richard Bergmair**
recipient of a DOC-fellowship of the Austrian Academy of Sciences
at the University of Cambridge Computer Laboratory;
15 JJ Thomson Avenue, Cambridge CB3 0FD, UK;
rbergmair@acm.org

**Abstract**

We outline problems with the interpretation of accuracy in the presence of bias, arguing that the issue is a particularly pressing concern for RTE evaluation. Furthermore, we argue that average precision scores are unsuitable for RTE, and should not be reported. We advocate mutual information as a new evaluation measure that should be reported in addition to accuracy and confidence-weighted score.

## 1 Introduction

We assume that the reader is familiar with the evaluation methodology employed in the RTE challenge.[1] We address the following three problems we currently see with this methodology.

1. The distribution of three-way gold standard labels is neither balanced nor representative of an application scenario. Yet, systems are rewarded for learning this artificial bias from training data, while there is no indication of whether they could learn a different bias.

2. The notion of confidence ranking is misleading in the context of evaluating a ranking by average precision. The criteria implicitly invoked on rankings by the current evaluation measures can, in fact, contradict those invoked on labellings derived by rank-based thresholding.

3. Language allows for the expression of logical negation, thus imposing a symmetry on the judgements ENTAILED vs. CONTRADICTION. Average precision does not properly reflect this symmetry.

In this paper, we will first summarize relevant aspects of the current methodology, and outline these three problems in greater depth.

[1] see the reports on RTE-1 (Dagan et al., 2005), RTE-2 (Bar-Haim et al., 2006), RTE-3 (Giampiccolo et al., 2007), the RTE-3 PILOT (Voorhees, 2008), RTE-4 (Giampicolo et al., 2008), and RTE-5 (TAC, 2009)

The problem of bias is quite general and widely known. Artstein and Poesio (2005) discuss it in the context of Cohen's kappa (Cohen, 1960), which is one way of addressing the problem. Yet, it has not received sufficient attention in the RTE community, which is why we will show how it applies to RTE, in particular, and why it is an especially pressing concern for RTE.

Average precision has been imported into the RTE evaluation methodology from IR, tacitly assuming a great level of analogy between IR and RTE. However, we will argue that the analogy is flawed, and that average precision is not suitable for RTE evaluation.

Then, we will then reframe the problem in information theoretic terms, advocating mutual information as a new evaluation measure. We will show that it addresses all of the issues raised concerning accuracy and average precision and has advantages over Cohen's kappa.

## 2 The Structure of RTE Data

Let $\mathcal{X}$ be the set of all candidate entailments that can be formed over a natural language of interest, such as English. An RTE dataset $\mathrm{X} \subseteq \mathcal{X}$ is a set of N candidate entailments $\mathrm{X} = \{\mathrm{x}_1, \mathrm{x}_2, \ldots, \mathrm{x}_\mathrm{N}\}$.

The RTE task is characterized as a classification task. A given candidate entailment $\mathrm{x}_i$ can be associated with either a positive class label $\triangle$ (TRUE / YES / ENTAILED) or a negative class label $\triangledown$ (FALSE / NO / NOT ENTAILED), but never both. In the three-way subtask, the positive class, which we will denote as $\boxplus$, is defined as before, but the negative class $\triangledown$ is further subdivided into a class $\boxminus$ (NO / CONTRADICTION) and a class $\Diamond$ (UNKNOWN). To model this subdivision, we define equivalence classes $[\cdot]_3$ and $[\cdot]_2$ on the three-way labels as follows: $[\boxplus]_3 = \boxplus$, $[\Diamond]_3 = \Diamond$, $[\boxminus]_3 = \boxminus$, $[\boxplus]_2 = \triangle$, $[\Diamond]_2 = \triangledown$, and $[\boxminus]_2 = \triangledown$.

The gold standard G for dataset X is then a labelling $\mathrm{G} : \mathrm{X} \mapsto \{\boxplus, \Diamond, \boxminus\}$. We call a candidate



*Proceedings of the 2009 Workshop on Applied Textual Inference, ACL-IJCNLP 2009*, pages 10–17,
Suntec, Singapore, 6 August 2009. 

entailment $x_i$ a $\triangle$-instance iff $[G(x_i)]_2 = \triangle$, and analogously for the other class labels.

The output $(L, \succ)$ of an RTE system on dataset X also contains such a labelling $L : X \mapsto \{\boxplus, \Diamond, \boxminus\}$, in addition to a strict total order $\succ$ on X representing a ranking of candidate entailments.

### 2.1 Logical Preliminaries

The notation chosen here is inspired by modal logic. Let's say a candidate entailment $x_i$ were of the logical form $\varphi \rightarrow \psi$. The formula "$\Box(\varphi \rightarrow \psi)$" would then assert that $\psi$ *necessarily* follows from $\varphi$ (ENTAILMENT), and the formula "$\Box(\varphi \rightarrow \neg\psi)$", which would be equivalent to "$\neg\Diamond(\varphi \wedge \psi)$", would mean that we can *not possibly* have $\varphi \wedge \psi$ (CONTRADICTION). We think of the former as a positive form of necessity ($\boxplus$), and of the latter as a negative form of necessity ($\boxminus$). The formula "$\Diamond(\varphi \rightarrow \psi)$" would assert that $\psi$ *possibly* follows from $\varphi$ (UNKNOWN).

We will have to assume that this negation operator $\neg$ is in fact within the expressive power of the natural language of interest, i.e. "$\varphi \rightarrow \neg\psi$" $\in \mathcal{X}$, whenever "$\varphi \rightarrow \psi$" $\in \mathcal{X}$. It imposes a symmetry on the two labels $\boxplus$ and $\boxminus$, with $\Diamond$ being neutral.

For example: *"Socrates is a man and every man is mortal; Therefore Socrates is mortal."* This candidate entailment is a $\boxplus$-instance. It corresponds to the following $\boxminus$-instance: *"Socrates is a man and every man is mortal; Therefore Socrates is not mortal"*. But then, consider the $\Diamond$-instance *"Socrates is mortal; Therefore Socrates is a man"*. Here *"Socrates is mortal; Therefore Socrates is not a man"* is still a $\Diamond$-instance.

It is this modal logic interpretation which matches most closely the ideas conveyed by the task definitions (TAC, 2009), and the annotation guidelines (de Marneffe and Manning, 2007). However, for the two-way task, they allude more to probabilistic logic or fuzzy logic, where a candidate entailment is a $\triangle$-instance iff it holds to a higher degree or likelihood or probability than its negation, and a $\nabla$-instance otherwise.

We believe that either a three-way modal logic entailment task or a two-way probabilistic logic entailment task on its own could make perfect sense. However, they are qualitatively different and not trivially related by equating $\triangle$ with $\boxplus$, and subdividing $\nabla$ into $\Diamond$ and $\boxminus$.

## 3 Accuracy & Related Measures

Both the system and the gold standard apply to the dataset X a total labelling L and G respectively, i.e. they are forced to assign their best guess label to every instance. A degree of agreement can be determined as a percentage agreement either on the two-way or the three-way distinction:

$$\mathbb{A}_3(L; G) = \frac{1}{N}\sum_{i=1}^{N} \mathbb{1}([L(x_i)]_3 = [G(x_i)]_3),$$

$$\mathbb{A}_2(L; G) = \frac{1}{N}\sum_{i=1}^{N} \mathbb{1}([L(x_i)]_2 = [G(x_i)]_2),$$

where $\mathbb{1}$ is a counter which takes on a numerical value of one, when the logical expression in its argument is true, and zero otherwise.

The RTE-3 PILOT (Voorhees, 2008) reported some accuracy measures conditioned on gold standard labels as follows:

$$\mathbb{A}'_3(L; G, g) = \frac{\sum_{i=1}^{N} \mathbb{1}([L(x_i)]_3 = [G(x_i)]_3 = g)}{\sum_{i=1}^{N} \mathbb{1}([G(x_i)]_3 = g)},$$

$$\mathbb{A}'_2(L; G, g) = \frac{\sum_{i=1}^{N} \mathbb{1}([L(x_i)]_2 = [G(x_i)]_2 = g)}{\sum_{i=1}^{N} \mathbb{1}([G(x_i)]_2 = g)}.$$

Assuming the usual analogy with IR, we note that $\mathbb{A}'_2(L; G, \triangle)$ is akin to recall. On the other hand, $\mathbb{A}'_2(G; L, \triangle)$, which conditions accuracy on the system-assigned labels rather than the gold standard labels, is precision.

The conditioned accuracy measures do not provide a single summary statistic as the others do. However, such a summary could be defined by taking the mean across the different labels:

$$\mathbb{A}'_3(L; G) = \frac{1}{3} \sum_{g \in \{\boxplus, \Diamond, \boxminus\}} \mathbb{A}'_3(L; G; g),$$

$$\mathbb{A}'_2(L; G) = \frac{1}{2} \sum_{g \in \{\triangle, \nabla\}} \mathbb{A}'_2(L; G; g).$$

It is instructive to consider a number of trivial baseline systems. Let $S^{\boxplus}$, $S^{\Diamond}$, and $S^{\boxminus}$, be the systems that uniformly assign to everything the labels $\boxplus$, $\Diamond$, and $\boxminus$, respectively, so that for all $i$: $L^{\boxplus}(x_i) = \boxplus$, $L^{\Diamond}(x_i) = \Diamond$, and $L^{\boxminus}(x_i) = \boxminus$. Also consider system $S^*$, which assigns labels at random, according to a uniform distribution.

The performance of these systems depends on the distribution of gold-standard labels. The policy at RTE was to sample in such a way that the resulting two-way labels in the gold standard would be balanced. So 50% of all $i$ had $[\mathrm{G}(\mathrm{x}_i)]_2 = \triangle$, while the other 50% had $[\mathrm{G}(\mathrm{x}_i)]_2 = \triangledown$.

This means that all trivial baselines have an accuracy of $\mathbb{A}_2 = \mathbb{A}'_2 = 50\%$. If the data were balanced on the three-way labels, which they are not, we would analogously have $\mathbb{A}_3 = \mathbb{A}'_3 = 33\%$.

When interpreting a two-way accuracy, one would thus expect values between $50\%$ and $100\%$, where $50\%$ indicates a trivial system and $100\%$ indicates a perfect system. A value of, for example, $70\%$ could be interpreted as-is, mindful of the above range restriction, or the range restriction could be factored into the value by using a linear transformation. One would then say that the accuracy of $70\%$ is $40\%$ of the way into the relevant range of $50\% - 100\%$, and quote the value as a Cohen's Kappa of $\kappa = 0.4$.

### 3.1 Bias

While the RTE datasets are balanced on two-way gold standard labels, they are not balanced on the three-way gold standard labels. Among the candidate entailments $\mathrm{x}_i$ with $[\mathrm{G}(\mathrm{x}_i)]_2 = \triangledown$, in RTE-4, 70% of all $\mathrm{x}_i$ had $[\mathrm{G}(\mathrm{x}_i)]_3 = \Diamond$, while only 30% had $[\mathrm{G}(\mathrm{x}_i)]_3 = \boxminus$. In the RTE-3 PILOT, the distribution was even more skewed, at 82%/18%.

So, we observe that $\mathrm{S}^{\boxplus}$ has $\mathbb{A}_3(\mathrm{L}^{\boxplus}; \mathrm{G}) = .500$ and therefore outperforms two thirds of all RTE-3 PILOT participants and one third of all RTE-4 participants. On the other hand, only very few participants performed worse than the random choice system $\mathrm{S}^*$, which had $\mathbb{A}_3(\mathrm{L}^*; \mathrm{G}) = .394$ on RTE-4. The other trivial systems have $\mathbb{A}_3(\mathrm{L}^{\Diamond}; \mathrm{G}) = .350$, followed by $\mathbb{A}_3(\mathrm{L}^{\boxminus}; \mathrm{G}) = .150$ on RTE-4.

The conditioned accuracies seem to promise a way out, since they provide an artificial balance across the gold standard labels. We have $\mathbb{A}'_3(\mathrm{L}^{\boxplus}; \mathrm{G}) = \mathbb{A}'_3(\mathrm{L}^{\Diamond}; \mathrm{G}) = \mathbb{A}'_3(\mathrm{L}^{\boxminus}; \mathrm{G}) = .33$. But this measure is then counter-intuitive in that the random-choice system $\mathrm{S}^*$ gets $\mathbb{A}'_3(\mathrm{L}^*; \mathrm{G}) = .394$ on RTE-4 and would thus be considered strictly superior to the system $\mathrm{S}^{\boxplus}$, which, if nothing else, at least reproduces the right bias. Another caveat is that this would weigh errors on rare labels more heavily than errors on common labels.

In some form or another the problem of bias applies not only to accuracy itself, but also to related statistics, such as precision, recall, precision/recall curves, and confidence weighted score. It is therefore quite general, and there are three responses which are commonly seen:

1. For purposes of intrinsic evaluation, one can use samples that have been balanced artificially, as it is being done in the two-way RTE task. Yet, it is impossible to balance a dataset both on a two-way and a three-way labelling at the same time.

2. One can use representative samples and argue that the biased accuracies have an extrinsic interpretation. For example, in IR, precision is the probability that a document chosen randomly from the result set will be considered relevant by the user. Yet, for RTE, one cannot provide a representative sample, as the task is an abstraction over a number of different applications, such as information extraction (IE), question answering (QA), and summarization (SUM), all of which give rise to potentially very different distributions of labels.

3. On statistical grounds, one can account for the possibility of random agreement in the presence of bias using Cohen's kappa (Artstein and Poesio, 2005; Di Eugenio and Glass, 2004). We will outline mutual information as an alternative, arguing that it has additional advantages.

## 4 Average Precision

The purpose of average precision is to evaluate against the gold standard labelling G the system-assigned ranking $\succ$, rather than directly comparing the two labellings G and L.

This is done by deriving from the ranking $\succ$ a series of binary labellings. The $i$-th labelling in that series is that which labels all instances up to rank $i$ as $\triangle$. A precision value can be computed for each of these labellings, compared to the same gold standard, and then averaged.

More formally, $\succ$ is the strict total ordering on the dataset X which has been produced by the system. Let $\mathrm{x}_j \succeq \mathrm{x}_i$ iff $\mathrm{x}_j \succ \mathrm{x}_i$ or $\mathrm{x}_j = \mathrm{x}_i$. We can then associate with each instance $\mathrm{x}_i$ a numeric rank, according to its position in $\succ$:

$$\#_{\succ}(\mathrm{x}_i) = \sum_{j=1}^{\mathrm{N}} \mathbb{1}(\mathrm{x}_j \succeq \mathrm{x}_i).$$

We can then define the cutoff labelling $\succ^{(r)}$ as

$$\succ^{(r)}(\mathrm{x}_i) = \begin{cases} \triangle & \text{if } \#_{\succ}(\mathrm{x}_i) \leqslant r, \\ \triangledown & \text{otherwise;} \end{cases}$$

and average precision as

$$\mathbb{AP}(\mathrm{G}; \succ) = \frac{1}{\mathrm{N}} \sum_{r=1}^{\mathrm{N}} \mathbb{A}'_2\left(\mathrm{G}; \succ^{(r)}, \triangle\right).$$

The system-assigned labelling L and the series of ranking-based labellings $\succ^{(r)}$ are initially independent, but, since both accuracy and average precision refer to the same gold standard G, we get the following condition on how L must relate to $\succ$: We call a system output $(\mathrm{L}, \succ)$ sound if there exists a cutoff rank $r$, such that L equals $\succ^{(r)}$, and self-contradictory otherwise. This is because, for a self-contradictory system output, there does not exist a gold standard for which it would be perfect, in the sense that both accuracy and average precision would simultaneously yield a value of $100\%$.

So far, we avoided the common terminology referring to $\succ$ as a "confidence ranking", as the notion of confidence would imply that we force the system to give its best guess labels, but also allow it to provide a measure of confidence, in this case by ranking the instances, to serve as a modality for the interpretation of such a best guess.

This is not what is being evaluated by average precision. Here, a system can remain entirely ignorant as to what is a $\triangle$- or a $\triangledown$-instance. System-assigned labels do not enter the definition, and systems are not required to choose a cutoff $r$ to derive a labelling $\succ^{(r)}$. This sort of evaluation is adequate for IR purposes, where the system output is genuinely a ranking, and it is up to the user to set a cutoff on what is relevant to them. As for RTE, it is unclear to us whether this applies.

### 4.1 Thresholding

In the previous section, we have seen that it is somewhat misleading to see $\succ$ as a confidence-ranking on the labelling L. Here, we argue that, even worse than that, the interpretations of $\succ$ and L may contradict each other. It is impossible for a system to optimize its output $(\mathrm{L}, \succ)$ for accuracy $\mathbb{A}_2(\mathrm{G}; \mathrm{L})$ and simultaneously for average precision $\mathbb{AP}(\mathrm{G}; \succ)$, while maintaining as a side condition that the information state $(\mathrm{L}, \succ)$ remain sound at all times. We show this by indirect argument.

For the sake of contradiction, assume that the system has come up with an internal information state consisting of the ranking $\succ$ and the labelling L, as a best guess. Also assume that this information state is sound.

Let's assume furthermore, again for the sake of contradiction, that the system is now allowed to query an oracle with access to the gold standard in order to revise the internal information state with the goal of improving its performance as measured by accuracy, and simultaneously also improving its performance as measured by average precision.

First, the oracle reveals r, the number of $\triangle$-instances in the gold standard. Let instance $\mathrm{x_i}$ at rank $\#_{\succ}(\mathrm{x_i}) = \mathrm{r}$ be correctly classified, and the instance $\mathrm{x_j}$ at some rank $\#_{\succ}(\mathrm{x_j}) > \mathrm{r}+1$ be incorrectly classified. So we would have $[\mathrm{L}(\mathrm{x_i})]_2 = \mathrm{L}^{(\mathrm{r})}_{\succ}(\mathrm{x_i}) = [\mathrm{G}(\mathrm{x_i})]_2 = \triangle$, and $[\mathrm{L}(\mathrm{x_j})]_2 = \mathrm{L}^{(\mathrm{r})}_{\succ}(\mathrm{x_j}) = \triangledown \neq [\mathrm{G}(\mathrm{x_j})]_2$.

Next, the oracle reveals the fact that $\mathrm{x_j}$ had been misclassified. In response to that new information, the system could change the classification and set $\mathrm{L}(\mathrm{x_j}) \leftarrow \triangle$. This would lead to an increase in accuracy. Average precision would remain unaffected, as it is a function of $\succ$, not L.

However, the information state $(\mathrm{L}, \succ)$ is now self-contradictory. The ranking $\succ$ would have to be adapted as well to reflect the new information. Let's say $\mathrm{x_j}$ were reranked by inserting it at some rank $\mathrm{r'} \leqslant \mathrm{r}$. This would lead to all intervening instances, including $\mathrm{x_i}$, to be ranked down, and thus to an increase in average precision.

But, since $\mathrm{x_i}$ has now fallen below the threshold r, which was, by definition, the correct threshold chosen by the oracle, the system would reclassify it as $[\mathrm{L}(\mathrm{x_j})]_2 = \triangledown$, which now introduces a labelling error. While average precision would not react to this relabelling, accuracy would now drop.

So there are two rather counterintuitive conclusions concerning the simultaneous application of accuracy, average precision, and thresholding. First, accuracy may prefer self-contradictory outputs to sound outputs. Second, when soundness is being forced, average precision may prefer lower accuracy to higher accuracy labellings.

Again, it should be stressed that RTE is the only prominent evaluation scheme we know of that insists on this combination of accuracy and average precision. If we had used precision and average precision, as in IR, the above argument would not hold. Also, in IR, average precision clearly dominates other measures in its importance.

### 4.2 Logical Symmetry

Besides the above arguments on bias, and on the contradictions between accuracy and average precision under a thresholding interpretation, there is a third problem with the current evaluation methodology. It arises from the symmetry between the classes $\boxplus$ and $\boxminus$ which we introduced in section 2.1. This problem is a direct result of the inherent properties of language and logic, and is, thus, the argument which is most specific to RTE.

Let $X = \{x_1, x_2, \ldots, x_N\}$ be a dataset, and let

$$\neg X = \{\neg x_1, \neg x_2, \ldots, \neg x_N\}$$

be the dataset resulting from the application of negation to each of the candidate entailments. Similarly, let $G : X \mapsto \{\boxplus, \Diamond, \boxminus\}$ be a gold standard and for all $x \in X$, let

$$\neg G(\neg x) = \begin{cases} \boxminus & \text{if } G(x) = \boxplus, \\ \Diamond & \text{if } G(x) = \Diamond, \\ \boxplus & \text{if } G(x) = \boxminus, \end{cases}$$

and analogously for the system-assigned labels L.

Intuitively, we would now expect the following of an evaluation measure: A system that produces the labelling L for dataset X is equivalent, in terms of the evaluation measure, to a system that produces labelling $\neg L$ for dataset $\neg X$. This is indeed true for three-way accuracy, where $\mathbb{A}_3(G; L) = \mathbb{A}_3(\neg G; \neg L)$, but it is not true for two-way accuracy, where the three-way classes are now lumped together in a different way.

Also, this symmetry is not present in average precision, which looks only at positive instances. Since the set of $\triangle$-instances of X and the set of $\triangle$-instances of $\neg X$ are disjoint, the two average precisions $\mathbb{AP}(G; \succ)$ and $\mathbb{AP}(\neg G; \succ')$, regardless of how $\succ$ relates to $\succ'$, need not be functionally related. – This makes sense in IR, where the set of irrelevant and non-retrieved documents must not enter into the evaluation of a retrieval system. But it makes no sense for the RTE task, where we do need to evaluate systems on the ability to assign a single label to all and only the contradictory candidate entailments.

## 5 Mutual Information

In this section, we define mutual information as a possible new evaluation measure for RTE. In particular, we return to the problem of bias and show that, like Cohen's kappa, mutual information does not suffer from bias. We will then introduce a new problem, which we shall call degradation. We show that Cohen's kappa suffers from degradation, but mutual information does not. Finally, we will extend the discussion to account for confidence.

Recall that an RTE dataset is a set of N candidate entailments $X = \{x_1, x_2, \ldots, x_N\}$, and let $\mathbf{X}$ be a random variable representing the result of a random draw from this set. Let $\mathbb{P}(\mathbf{X} = x_i)$ be the probability that $x_i$ comes up in the draw. This could represent, for example, the prior probability that a particular question is asked in a question answering scenario. In the absence of any extrinsically defined interpretations, one could set random variable $\mathbf{X}$ to be uniformly distributed, i.e. $\mathbb{P}(\mathbf{X} = x_i) = \frac{1}{N}$ for all $i$.

This yields a number of further random variables: Let $\mathbf{G}$ and $\mathbf{L}$ be the label $G(x_i)$ and $L(x_i)$ respectively, assigned to the candidate $x_i$ which has been drawn at random. As usual, we will be interested in their joint distribution, and the resulting marginals and conditionals.

We give the remaining definitions leading to mutual information in Figure 1, and will discuss them by considering the particular contingency table in Figure 2 as an example. It also spells out the information theoretic calculations in detail. Furthermore, we will present corresponding values for Cohen's kappa, which should be easy for the reader to retrace, and thus have been omitted from the Figure for brevity.

The unconditional entropy $\mathbb{H}(\mathbf{G})$ serves as a convenient measure of the hardness of the classification task itself, taking into account the number of labels and their distribution in the gold standard. In the example, this distribution has been chosen to match that of the RTE-4 dataset almost precisely, yielding a value for $\mathbb{H}(\mathbf{G})$ of 1.4277 bits. This indicates that it is much harder to guess the three-way gold standard label of an RTE-4 candidate entailment than it is to guess the two-way label, or the outcome of a toss of a fair coin, which would both have an entropy of exactly 1 bit. On the other hand, due to the skewness of the distribution, it is easier to guess this outcome than it would be if the distribution was uniform, in which case we would have an entropy of 1.5850 bits.

Similarly, we can calculate a conditional entropy $\mathbb{H}(\mathbf{G}|\mathbf{L} = l)$ over a conditional distribution of gold standard labels observed, given that the system has assigned label $l$ to our randomly chosen candidate entailment. In the example, we have calculated a value of 1.0746 bits for $\mathbb{H}(\mathbf{G}|\mathbf{L} = \boxplus)$. So, while the hardness of guessing the correct label without any additional knowledge is 1.4277, it will be easier to guess this label correctly once the system-assigned label is known to be $\boxplus$.

Our best guess would be to always assign label $\boxplus$, which would be successful 50% of the time.

$$\mathbb{P}(\mathbf{G}=g,\mathbf{L}=l) = \sum_{i=1}^{\mathrm{N}} \mathbb{P}(\mathbf{X}=\mathrm{x}_i)\, \mathbb{1}\Big(\mathrm{G}(\mathrm{x}_i)=g \ \wedge\ \mathrm{L}(\mathrm{x}_i)=l\Big); \tag{1}$$

$$\mathbb{P}(\mathbf{G}=g) = \sum_{l} \mathbb{P}(\mathbf{G}=g,\mathbf{L}=l) \tag{2}$$

$$\mathbb{P}(\mathbf{L}=l) = \sum_{g} \mathbb{P}(\mathbf{G}=g,\mathbf{L}=l) \tag{3}$$

$$\mathbb{P}(\mathbf{G}=g|\mathbf{L}=l) = \frac{\mathbb{P}(\mathbf{G}=g,\mathbf{L}=l)}{\mathbb{P}(\mathbf{L}=l)}; \tag{4}$$

$$\mathbb{H}(\mathbf{G}) = -\sum_{g} \mathbb{P}(\mathbf{G}=g)\ \log\Big(\mathbb{P}(\mathbf{G}=g)\Big); \tag{5}$$

$$\mathbb{H}(\mathbf{G}|\mathbf{L}=l) = -\sum_{g} \mathbb{P}(\mathbf{G}=g|\mathbf{L}=l)\ \log\Big(\mathbb{P}(\mathbf{G}=g|\mathbf{L}=l)\Big); \tag{6}$$

$$\mathbb{H}(\mathbf{G}|\mathbf{L}) = \sum_{l} \mathbb{P}(\mathbf{L}=l)\ \mathbb{H}(\mathbf{G}|\mathbf{L}=l); \tag{7}$$

$$\mathbb{I}(\mathbf{G};\mathbf{L}) = \mathbb{H}(\mathbf{G}) - \mathbb{H}(\mathbf{G}|\mathbf{L}). \tag{8}$$

Figure 1: definitions for mutual information $\mathbb{I}(\mathbf{G};\mathbf{L})$

| | | | |
|---|---|---|---|
| 20 (45) | 25 (0) | 5 | $\mathbb{P}(\mathrm{G}=\boxplus) = .5$ |
| 9 (27) | 18 (0) | 9 | $\mathbb{P}(\mathrm{G}=\Diamond) = .36$ |
| 1 (8) | 7 (0) | 6 | $\mathbb{P}(\mathrm{G}=\boxminus) = .14$ |
| $\mathbb{P}(\mathrm{L}=\boxplus) = .3$ (.8) | $\mathbb{P}(\mathrm{L}=\Diamond) = .5$ (0) | $\mathbb{P}(\mathrm{L}=\boxminus) = .2$ (.2) | N = 100 |

$$\begin{aligned} -\mathbb{H}(\mathbf{G}) &= .5\ \log_2(.5) \\ &+ .36\ \log_2(.36) \\ &+ .14\ \log_2(.14) \\ &= -1.4277 \end{aligned}$$

$$\begin{aligned} -\mathbb{H}(\mathbf{G}|\mathbf{L}=\boxplus) &= \frac{20}{30}\ \log_2(\frac{20}{30}) \\ &+ \frac{9}{30}\ \log_2(\frac{9}{30}) \\ &+ \frac{1}{30}\ \log_2(\frac{1}{30}) \\ &= -1.0746 \end{aligned}$$

$$\begin{aligned} -\mathbb{H}(\mathbf{G}|\mathbf{L}=\Diamond) &= \frac{25}{50}\ \log_2(\frac{25}{50}) \\ &+ \frac{18}{50}\ \log_2(\frac{18}{50}) \\ &+ \frac{7}{50}\ \log_2(\frac{7}{50}) \\ &= -1.4277 \end{aligned}$$

$$\begin{aligned} -\mathbb{H}(\mathbf{G}|\mathbf{L}=\boxminus) &= \frac{5}{20}\ \log_2(\frac{5}{20}) \\ &+ \frac{9}{20}\ \log_2(\frac{9}{20}) \\ &+ \frac{6}{20}\ \log_2(\frac{6}{20}) \\ &= -1.5395 \end{aligned}$$

$$\begin{aligned} \mathbb{H}(\mathbf{G}|\mathbf{L}) &= .3 * 1.0746 \\ &+ .5 * 1.4277 \\ &+ .2 * 1.5395 \\ &= 1.3441 \end{aligned}$$

$$\begin{aligned} -\mathbb{H}(\mathbf{G}|\mathbf{L}'=\boxplus) &= \frac{45}{80}\ \log_2(\frac{45}{80}) \\ &+ \frac{27}{80}\ \log_2(\frac{27}{80}) \\ &+ \frac{8}{80}\ \log_2(\frac{8}{80}) \\ &= -1.3280 \end{aligned}$$

$$\begin{aligned} \mathbb{H}(\mathbf{G}|\mathbf{L}') &= .8 * 1.3280 \\ &+ .2 * 1.5395 \\ &= 1.3703 \end{aligned}$$

Figure 2: example contingency table and entropy calculations

But, among the cases where the system in Figure 2 has assigned label $\boxplus$, this would be an even better guess. It would now be correct $66\%$ of the time. We have gained information about the gold standard by looking at the system-assigned label.

### 5.1 Bias

The conditional entropy $\mathbb{H}(\mathbf{G}|\mathbf{L})$ is the expected value of the conditional entropy $\mathbb{H}(\mathbf{G}|\mathbf{L} = l)$ across all possible labels $l$, when, as before, we draw a candidate entailment at random.

One very noteworthy property of this measure is that all of the baseline systems we considered, i.e. systems assigning constant labels, or systems assigning labels at random, would have $\mathbb{H}(\mathbf{G}|\mathbf{L}) = \mathbb{H}(\mathbf{G})$, since the distribution of gold standard labels given the system labels, in all of these cases, is the same as the prior distribution. Furthermore, $\mathbb{H}(\mathbf{G}) = 1.4277$ is, in fact, an upper bound on $\mathbb{H}(\mathbf{G}|\mathbf{L})$. All the trivial baseline systems would perform at this upper bound level.

At the other extreme end of the spectrum, consider a perfect contingency table, where all the non-diagonal cells are zero. In this case all the conditional entropies $\mathbb{H}(\mathbf{G}|\mathbf{L} = l)$ would be entropies over delta distributions concentrating all probability mass on a single label. This would yield a value of $\mathbb{H}(\mathbf{G}|\mathbf{L}) = 0$, which is a lower bound for any entropy. – For Cohen's kappa we would have $\kappa = 1$.

The system producing our contingency table performs worse than this ideal but better than the baselines, at $\mathbb{H}(\mathbf{G}|\mathbf{L}) = 1.3441$. One can subtract $\mathbb{H}(\mathbf{G}|\mathbf{L})$ from the upper bound $\mathbb{H}(\mathbf{G})$ to obtain the mutual information $\mathbb{I}(\mathbf{G};\mathbf{L})$. It is the information gained about $\mathbf{G}$ once the value of $\mathbf{L}$ is revealed. It is obviously still bounded between 0 and $\mathbb{H}(\mathbf{G})$, but is somewhat more intuitive as an evaluation measure, as it restores the basic intuition that larger values indicate higher performance. – Due to a surprising result of information theory it also turns out that $\mathbb{I}(\mathbf{G};\mathbf{L}) = \mathbb{I}(\mathbf{L};\mathbf{G})$. This symmetry is another property one would intuitively expect when comparing two labellings G and L to each other, and is also present for accuracy and kappa.

We can compare the behaviour of this measure to that of accuracy. The accuracy of our example system is simply the sum of the diagonal contingency counts, so it scores at $44\%$, compared to $50\%$ for the baseline that always assigns label $\boxplus$. The new bias-aware framework provides a quite different point of view. We would now note that the example system does provide $\mathbb{I}(\mathbf{L};\mathbf{G}) = 0.0836$ bits worth of information about $\mathbf{G}$, showing an agreement of $\kappa = 0.1277$, compared to zero information and $\kappa = 0$ agreement for the baseline.

### 5.2 Degradation

The numbers in the example have been chosen so as to illustrate a problem we call degradation. The conditional distribution $\mathbb{P}(\mathbf{G} = g|\mathbf{L} = \Diamond)$ is the same as the unconditional distribution $\mathbb{P}(\mathbf{G} = g)$, so when it turns out that $\mathbf{L} = \Diamond$, no additional information has been revealed about $\mathbf{G}$. But in information theoretic terms, it is considered good to know when exactly we know nothing.

What happens if we conflate the labels $\Diamond$ and $\boxplus$ in the system output? In Figure, 2, the numbers in brackets illustrate this. Previously, the system assigned label $\boxplus$ in $30\%$ of all cases. In those cases, the system's choice was relatively well-informed, as $\boxplus$ actually turned out to be the correct gold standard label $66\%$ of the time. But now, with the labels conflated, the system chooses $\boxplus$ in $80\%$ of the cases; a choice which is now much less well-informed, as it is correct only $45\%$ of the time.

Mutual information shows a drop from $0.0836$ bits down to $0.0262$. On the other hand, accuracy increases from $44\%$ to $51\%$, and Cohen's kappa also increases from $0.1277$ to $0.1433$. But this is clearly counter-intuitive. Surely, it must be a bad thing to conflate a well-informed label with a less well-informed label, thus obscuring the output to less certainty and more guesswork.

### 5.3 Confidence Ranking

One final issue that has still remained unaddressed is that of confidence ranking. This takes us back to the very first probabilistic notion we introduced, that of a probability distribution $\mathbb{P}(\mathbf{X} = \mathrm{x}_i)$ governing the choice of the test-instances $\mathrm{x}_i$. The uniform distribution we suggested earlier results in all instances carrying equal weight in the evaluation.

But for some applications, it makes sense to give the system some control over which test-instances it wants to be tested on, independently of the question of what results it produces for that test. – So, from a probabilistic point of view, the most natural take on confidence would be to have the system itself output the values $\mathbb{P}(\mathbf{X} = \mathrm{x}_i)$ as confidence weights.

This would affect $\mathbb{H}(\mathbf{G})$, which we previously introduced as a measure of the difficulty of the task faced by the system. But now, the system has some control over what task it wants to try and solve. In an extreme scenario, it could concentrate all its confidence mass in a single instance. Another system might force itself to give equal weight to every instance. Clearly, these are two very different scenarios, so it seems natural that, as soon as the issue of confidence enters the scene, the evaluation has to consider two dimensions. The unconditional entropy $\mathbb{H}(\mathbf{G})$ would have to be reported for every system, together with the mutual information $\mathbb{I}(\mathbf{L};\mathbf{G})$. While $\mathbb{H}(\mathbf{G})$ would measure how effective a system was at using its confidence weighting as a tool to make the task easier on itself, $\mathbb{I}(\mathbf{L};\mathbf{G})$ would measure how successful the system ultimately was at the task it set for itself.

The example of a system concentrating all of its confidence mass in a single instance shows that the ability to freely choose $\mathbb{P}(\mathbf{X} = \mathrm{x}_i)$ might not fit with realistic application scenarios. This leads to the idea of confidence ranking, where a system could only rank, not weigh, its decisions, and it would be up to the evaluation framework to then assign weights according to the ranks.

For example, one could let

$$\mathbb{P}(\mathbf{X} = \mathrm{x}_i) = \frac{\mathrm{N} + 1 - \#_{>}(\mathrm{x}_i)}{(\mathrm{N}+1) * (\mathrm{N}/2)}.$$

This would assign a weight of N to the highest-ranked instance, a weight of $\mathrm{N} - 1$ to the next, and continue in this manner down to the instance at rank N, which would get weight 1. The denominator in the above expression then serves to normalize this weighting to a probability distribution. Note that, in principle, nothing speaks against using any other series of weights. Perhaps further investigation into the application scenarios of RTE systems will provide an extrinsically motivated choice for such a confidence weighting.

## 6 Final Recommendations

Ultimately, our proposal boils down to four points, which we believe are well-supported by the evidence presented throughout this paper:

1. Additional clarification is needed as to the logical definitions of the two-way and the three-way distinction of entailment classes.

2. Accuracy and related evaluation measures suffer from bias, and thus scores of theoretical baselines must be reported and compared to system scores. These include random choice and choice of a constant label.

3. Average precision scores are misleading and should not be reported. The confidence-weighted score that has been dropped after RTE-1 would be preferable to average precision, but still suffers from bias.

4. Mutual information should be reported, in addition to accuracy and possibly confidence-weighted score, to account for bias and the degradation problem.

## Acknowledgments

I would like to thank the anonymous reviewers and my colleague Ekaterina Shutova for providing many helpful comments and my supervisor Ann Copestake for reading multiple drafts of this paper and providing a great number of suggestions within a very short timeframe. All errors and omissions are, of course, entirely my own. I gratefully acknowledge financial support by the Austrian Academy of Sciences.

## References

Ron Artstein and Massimo Poesio. 2005. Kappa3 = alpha (or beta). Technical Report CSM-437, University of Essex Department of Computer Science.

Roy Bar-Haim, Ido Dagan, Bill Dolan, Lisa Ferro, Danilo Giampiccolo, Bernardo Magnini, and Idan Szpektor. 2006. The second pascal recognising textual entailment challenge. In *Proceedings of the Second PASCAL Challenges Workshop on Recognising Textual Entailment (RTE-2)*.

Jacob Cohen. 1960. A coefficient of agreement for nominal scales. *Educational and Psychological Measurement*, 20:37–46.

Ido Dagan, Oren Glickman, and Bernardo Magnini. 2005. The pascal recognising textual entailment challenge. In Ido Dagan, Oren Glickman, and Bernardo Magnini, editors, *Proceedings of the PASCAL Challenges Workshop on Recognising Textual Entailment (RTE-1)*.

Marie-Catherine de Marneffe and Christopher Manning. 2007. Contradiction annotation. http:// nlp.stanford.edu/ RTE3-pilot/ contradictions.pdf.

Barbara Di Eugenio and Michael Glass. 2004. The kappa statistic: A second look. *Computational Linguistics*, 30(1):95–101.

Danilo Giampiccolo, Bernardo Magnini, Ido Dagan, and Bill Dolan. 2007. The third pascal recognising textual entailment challenge. In *Proceedings of the Workshop on Textual Entailment and paraphrasing (RTE-3)*.

Danilo Giampicolo, Hoa Trang Dang, Bernardo Magnini, Ido Dagan, and Bill Dolan. 2008. The fourth pascal recognizing textual entailment challenge. In *Preproceedings of the Text Analysis Conference (TAC)*.

TAC. 2009. Tac2009 rte-5 main task guidelines. http:// www.nist.gov/ tac/ 2009/ RTE/ RTE5_Main_Guidelines.pdf.

Ellen M. Voorhees. 2008. Contradictions and justifications: Extensions to the textual entailment task. In *Proceedings of ACL-08: HLT*, pages 63–71.

# Sub-sentential Paraphrasing by Contextual Pivot Translation

**Aurélien Max**
LIMSI-CNRS
Université Paris-Sud 11
Orsay, France
aurelien.max@limsi.fr

## Abstract

The ability to generate or to recognize paraphrases is key to the vast majority of NLP applications. As correctly exploiting context during translation has been shown to be successful, using context information for paraphrasing could also lead to improved performance. In this article, we adopt the pivot approach based on parallel multilingual corpora proposed by (Bannard and Callison-Burch, 2005), which finds short paraphrases by finding appropriate pivot phrases in one or several auxiliary languages and back-translating these pivot phrases into the original language. We show how context can be exploited both when attempting to find pivot phrases, and when looking for the most appropriate paraphrase in the original subsentential "envelope". This framework allows the use of paraphrasing units ranging from words to large sub-sentential fragments for which context information from the sentence can be successfully exploited. We report experiments on a text revision task, and show that in these experiments our contextual sub-sentential paraphrasing system outperforms a strong baseline system.

## 1 Introduction

The ability to generate or to recognize paraphrases is key to the vast majority of NLP applications. Most current research efforts on paraphrase generation attempt to push the limits of their respective methods and resources without recourse to deep meaning interpretation, an admitedly long-term research objective. A step towards meaning-aware paraphrasing can be done by appropriate use of the context in which a paraphrasing occurrence occurs. At the lowest level, deciding automatically when a word can be substituted with a synonym is a complex issue (Connor and Roth, 2007). When attempting paraphrasing on a higher level, such as arbitrary phrases or full sentences (Barzilay and Lee, 2003; Pang et al., 2003; Quirk et al., 2004; Bannard and Callison-Burch, 2005; Zhao et al., 2008a), a first issue concerns the acquisition of elementary units, which in the general case do not exist in predefined dictionaries. Some paraphrasing strategy must then follow, which may consider the context of a substitution to guide the selection of appropriate units (Callison-Burch, 2008; Max, 2008). An important limitation to this family of works is the scarcity of corpora that can be used as reliable supervised training data. Indeed, strictly parallel sentence pairs, for instance, are not naturally produced in human activities.[1] As a consequence, works on paraphrasing have recourse to costly human evaluation procedures, and an objective of automatic evaluation metrics is to rely on as little gold standard data as possible (Callison-Burch et al., 2008).

A text revision task is an application of paraphrase generation where context may be used in an effective way. When a local change is made to a text, it occurs within a textual "envelope" within which a paraphrase should fit. In particular, if the original sentence was grammatical, the substituted sentence should remain grammatical and convey essentially the same meaning.[2] The manner in which such a context can be exploited depends of course on the type of automatic paraphrasing technique used. In this article, we adopt the pivot

[1] Recent works such as (Nelken and Yamangil, 2008) have proposed mining the revision histories of collaborative authoring resources like Wikipedia, offering interesting prospects in paraphrasing and rewriting studies.

[2] We posit here that the *revision* activity does not involve important semantic changes, as opposed to the *rewriting* activity. In future work, we will attempt to consider cases of paraphrasing involving meaning changes corresponding to textual entailment phenomena.



*Proceedings of the 2009 Workshop on Applied Textual Inference, ACL-IJCNLP 2009*, pages 18–26,
Suntec, Singapore, 6 August 2009. 

approach based on parallel multilingual corpora proposed by (Bannard and Callison-Burch, 2005), which finds short paraphrases by finding appropriate pivot phrases in one or several auxiliary languages and back-translating these pivot phrases into the original language. We show how context can be exploited both when attempting to find pivot phrases, and when looking for the most appropriate paraphrase in the original sub-sentential envelope. This framework allows the use of paraphrasing units ranging from words to large sub-sentential fragments for which context information from the sentence can be successfully exploited.

This article is organized as follows. In section 2, we briefly review related work in paraphrasing and context-aware Machine Translation. We describe the main characteristics of our approach to sub-sentential paraphrasing in section 3. We then describe an evaluation protocol for evaluating our proposal and report the results of a human evaluation in section 4. We finally conclude and present our future work in section 5.

## 2 Related work

Different sources have been considered for paraphrase acquisition techniques. (Pang et al., 2003), for example, apply syntactic fusion to multiple translations of individual sentences. (Barzilay and Lee, 2003; Dolan et al., 2004) acquire short paraphrases from comparable corpora, while (Bhagat and Ravichandran, 2008) considered the issue of acquiring short paraphrase patterns from huge amounts of comparable corpora. (Bannard and Callison-Burch, 2005) introduced a pivot approach to acquire short paraphrases from multilingual parallel corpora, a resource much more readily available than their monolingual counterpart. (Zhao et al., 2008b) acquire paraphrase patterns from bilingual corpora and report the various types obtained.[3] (Callison-Burch, 2008) improves the pivot paraphrase acquisition technique by using syntactic constraints at the level of constituents during phrase extraction. This works also uses syntactic constraints during phrase substitution, resulting in improvements in both grammaticality and meaning preservation in a large-scale experiment on English. (Max, 2008) explored the use of syntactic dependency preservation during phrase substitution on French.

This family of works considered the acquisition of short paraphrases and their use in local paraphrasing of known units. Several works have tackled full sentence paraphrasing as a monolingual translation task relying on Statistical Machine Translation (SMT). For instance, (Quirk et al., 2004) used a phrase-based SMT decoder that uses local paraphrases acquired from comparable corpora to produce monotone sentential paraphrases. (Zhao et al., 2008a) acquired monolingual biphrases from various sources and used them with a phrase-based SMT decoder, and (Madnani et al., 2007) combined rules of their hierarchical decoders by pivot to obtain a monolingual grammar. These works were not motivated by the generation of high-quality paraphrases that could, for example, be reused in documents. The lack of structural information, the local nature of the paraphrasing performed and the fact that the context of the original sentences was not taken into account in the phrase-based approaches make it difficult to control meaning preservation during paraphrasing.

Context has been shown to play a crucial role in Machine Translation, where in particular proper Word Sense Disambiguation (WSD) is required in many cases. A variety of works have integrated context with some success into phrase-based and hierarchical decoders. For example, (Carpuat and Wu, 2007) disambiguate phrases using a state-of-the-art WSD classifier, and (Stroppa et al., 2007) use a global memory-based classifier to find appropriate phrase translations in context. Context is often defined as local linguistic features such as surrounding words and their part-of-speech, but some works have experimented with more syntactic features (e.g. (Gimpel and Smith, 2008; Max et al., 2008; Haque et al., 2009)).

Using an intermediate pivot language with bilingual translation in which a given language pair is low-resourced has led to improvements in translation performance (Wu and Wang, 2007; Bertoldi et al., 2008), but to our knowledge this approach has not been applied to full sentence paraphrasing. Several reasons may explain this, in particular the relative low quality of current MT approaches on full sentence translation, and the difficulties in controlling what is paraphrased and how.

[3] The types of their paraphrase patterns are the following (numbers in parentheses indicate frequency in their database): phrase replacements (267); trivial changes (79); structural paraphrases (71); phrase reorderings (56); and addition of deletion of information that are claimed to not alter meaning (27).

## 3 Contextual pivot SMT for sub-sentential paraphrasing

Although many works have addressed the issue of local paraphrase acquisition, effective use of such paraphrases for paraphrase generation has only be achieved at the level of text units corresponding to short contiguous phrases. Recent works have proposed approaches to exploit context in order to correctly replace a text fragment with a paraphrase, but they are limited to known text units and therefore suffer from a scarcity of data.[4]

In this work, we address the case of sub-sentential paraphrase generation, an intermediate case between local paraphrasing using text units for which paraphrases are available and full sentence paraphrasing. Data sparcity is addressed by using a pivot translation mechanism, which can produce back-translations for text fragments for which paraphrases cannot be acquired beforehand by some paraphrase acquisition technique. Sub-sentential paraphrasing by pivot allows the exploitation of context during both source-to-pivot translation, where the source context is available, and during pivot-to-source back-translation, where the target context is known. The success of this approach is then directly dependent on the availability of high quality MT engines and on their ability to exploit these source and target contexts.

### 3.1 Paraphrasing by pivot translation

Whereas attempts at using two translation systems in pivot have met with some success for low-resourced language pairs, it is unlikely that current SMT systems can be successfully called in succession to obtain high-quality sentential paraphrases.[5] Several works have shown that monolingual biphrases obtained by multilingual pivots can be used by decoders, but although gains can for example be obtained by using sentential paraphrases as alternative reference corpora for optimizing SMT systems (Madnani et al., 2007), resulting paraphrases seem to be of too low quality for most other possible application contexts. In this work, we propose to use a pivot approach from a source language to a pivot language and back to the source language, but for sub-sentential fragments. In this way, the source context in which they occur can be exploited for both translating into the pivot language and for back-translating into the original language. This is illustrated on Figure 1.

Step (1) performs a $N$-best decoding (a single example is shown here) in which a segmentation of the source sentence is forced to ensure that a given fragment (*mettre en danger la richesse écologique* in the example) is translated independently of its surrounding context.[6] Only translations which respect this segmentation are kept, yielding a variety of pivot sentences. We are mostly interested in the pivot translation of our paraphrased fragment, but its prefix and suffix pivot context can be exploited by contextual SMT to guide pivot-to-source translation, although the lower quality of automatically generated sentences might not help as much as before.

Step (2) produces from each obtained $N$-best hypothesis a new $N$-best list of hypotheses, this time in the source language. The decoder is once more asked to use a given segmentation, and is further given imposed translations for the pivot prefix and suffix, as shown by the arrows going directly from the sentence at the top to the sentence at the bottom of Figure 1. Step (2) can be followed by a reranking procedure on the obtained $N$-best list of hypotheses, whose individual score can be obtained by combining the scores of the two translation hypotheses that led to it. As opposed to the pivot approach for phrases of (Bannard and Callison-Burch, 2005), it is not possible to sum over all possible pivots for a given pair $\langle$original sentence, paraphrased sentence$\rangle$, as the search space would make this computation impractical. We can instead look for the paraphrase that maximizes the product of the probabilities of the two translation steps according to the scores produced by the decoders used.

A further step can eliminate paraphrases by applying heuristics designed to define sought or undesirable properties for paraphrases, although this

[4]Current approaches based on paraphrase patterns are only a partial solution to this issue, as the variables used are limited to simple types.

[5]In particular, back-translation can introduce lexical errors due to incorrect word sense disambiguation and therefore severely hamper understanding, as illustrated by the infamous MT textbook example of the sentence *The spirit is willing but the flesh is weak* being translated into Russian and back-translated into English as *The vodka is good, but the meat is rotten.*

[6]It is in fact incorrect to say that translation of the various fragments would take place independently of each other, as various models such as a source context models or target language models will use information from surrounding fragments.

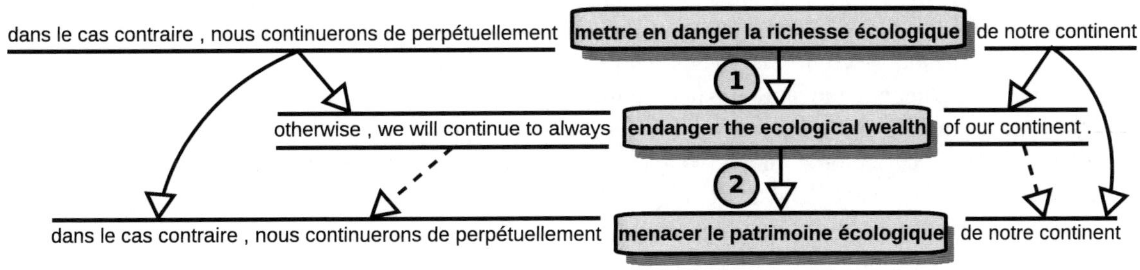


Figure 1: Example of sub-sentential paraphrasing by contextual pivot translation

could be directly integrated in the reranking step. For example, we may not be interested by identity paraphrases, or by paraphrases including or being included in the original fragment, or we may prefer paraphrases in which a given word has been replaced, etc.

## 3.2 Source context for pivot SMT

Using the context of a phrase is necessary to translate it correctly, most notably when several word senses corresponding to distinct translations are involved. The following examples show a case of a polysemous English word, which can be translated into three distinct French words and back-translated into various English fragments:

- *Follow the instructions outlined below to **save** that file. → sauvegarder ce fichier → write the file on disk*
- *Quitting smoking is a sure-fire way to **save** some money → économiser de l'argent → have some money on your bank account*
- *Brown's gamble may **save** the banks but the economy cannot wait. → sauver les banques → salvage the banks*

Our approach for source context aware SMT, based on that of (Stroppa et al., 2007), is illustrated by the system architecture on Figure 2. A memory-based classification approach was chosen as it allows for efficient training with large example sets, can handle any number of output classes and produces results that can be directly used to estimate the required conditional probabilities. We add context-informed features to the log-linear framework of our SMT system based on the conditional probability of a target phrase $e_i$ given a source phrase $f_i$ and its context, $C(f_i)$:

$h_m(f_i, C(f_i), e_i) = \log P(e_i | f_i, C(f_i))$

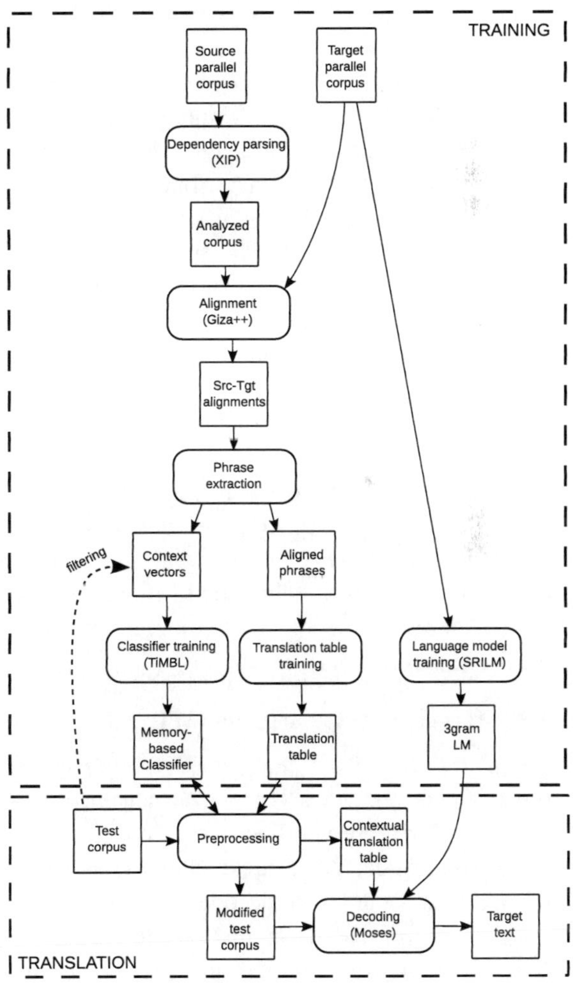


Figure 2: Architecture of our contextual phrase-based SMT system

Memory-based classification performs implicit smoothing, which addresses in part the problem of data sparcity, which worsen with the inclusion of context features and makes direct estimation of those probabilities problematic. Given a fixed-length vector, $\langle f_i, C(f_i)\rangle$, a set of weighted class labels corresponding to target phrases is returned by the classifier, which give access to $P(e_i|f_i, C(f_i))$ after normalization.

Because each source phrase potentially occurs in a unique context, they must be given a unique entry in the phrase table. To this end, we added a preprocessor component whose role is to dynamically build a modified source file containing unique tokens and to produce a modified translation table containing those tokens. Phrase extraction uses both phrase alignment results and linguistic analysis of the source corpus to produce standard biphrases and biphrases with contextual information. The latter are used to train the memory-based classifier. The source file undergoes the same linguistic analysis whose output is then aligned to unique tokens (e.g. president@45), and each possible phrase which is also present in the standard translation table is classified using its context information. The output is used to create a set of entries in the contextual translation tables, in which a new score corresponding to our context-based feature are added.

Most existing context-aware SMT approaches rely on context features from the immediate context of a source phrase. In this work, we initially restricted ourselves to a limited set of features: up to two lemmas to the left and to the right of a segment and their part-of-speech.[7]

### 3.3 Target context for pivot SMT

When decoding from the pivot hypothesis, we force our decoder to use provided sentence prefix and suffix corresponding to the "envelope" of the original fragment. Target context will thus be taken into account by the decoder.

Furthermore, based on the hypothesis that a paraphrase for an unmodified envelope should preserve the syntactic dependencies between the paraphrased fragment and its envelope (*inter-fragment dependencies*), we optionaly add a "hard" reranking step where we filter the $N$-best list of hypotheses to keep only those which preserve these dependencies. Note however that for a dependency to be marked as preserved, we only need to find its label and its target word in the envelope (governor or dependent), as the word in the paraphrased fragment might have changed. This of course has practical implications on the nature of the paraphrases that can be produced.

In part due to various deficiencies of phrase alignments discussed in (Callison-Burch, 2008), we further apply heuristics to filter out some undesirable paraphrase candidates. Our current set of heuristics includes:

- no reordering should have taken place between the original source phrase and its context[8];
- considering the set of full word lemmas for the original fragment and the paraphrased fragment, at least one lemma should not belong to both sets[9];
- neither the original fragment nor its paraphrase must be included into the other (only taking full words into account).

## 4 Experiments

We have conducted experiments motivated by a text revision task that we report in this section by describing our baseline and context-aware sub-sentential paraphrasing systems and the results of a small-scale manual evaluation.

### 4.1 Data and systems

We built two-way French-English SMT systems using 188,115 lines of the Europarl corpus (Koehn, 2005) of parliamentary debates with moses (Koehn et al., 2007) [10]. Our corpus was analyzed by the XIP robust parser (Aït-Mokhtar et al., 2002) and its output tokenization was used. We built standard systems, as well as a contextual system for French→English as described in section 3.2 using an additional contextual score ob-

[7]We will integrate richer syntactic context as in (Gimpel and Smith, 2008; Max et al., 2008) in our short-term future work, as we expect it to be particularly useful for our paraphrasing task.

[8]Reordering is allowed in the paraphrased fragment.

[9]As a consequence, minimal paraphrases may differ by only one full word. This can however be used advantageously when the sought type of paraphrasing aims at "normalizing" a text fragment and when the most appropriate rewording is very similar to an original text fragment.

[10]We used revision 2234 available on the moses SVN website: `http://mosesdecoder.sourceforge.net/svn.php`. In particular, it allows the use of XML annotations to guide the translation of particular fragments.

| | |
|---|---|
| Baseline fr→en | 30.56 |
| Contextual fr→en | 31.17 |
| Baseline en→fr | 32.10 |

Table 1: BLEU scores for the translation systems used by our paraphrasing system

tained through memory-based classification performed with the TiMBL package (Daelemans et al., 2007). Standard MERT was used to optimize model weights. BLEU scores for the three systems are reported on Table 1. The contextual system obtains a slightly higher score than the baseline system, which can participate to some extent to a better exploitation of context for paraphrasing.[11]

Two paraphrasing systems we built: $S_{bas}$ is a baseline system which uses standard phrase tables and post-filtering heuritics, but does not include reranking based on syntactic dependencies. $S_{cont}$ is a contextual system which uses the contextual French→English translation system, reranking based on syntactic dependencies and post-filtering heuristics.

We used 1000-best lists of hypotheses for the source-to-pivot translation, and restricted ourselves to much smaller 10-best lists for pivot-to-source translation (integrating early more constraints directly into decoding could help in obtaining better and smaller $N$-best lists).[12]

### 4.2 Evaluation protocol

A native speaker was asked to study a held-out test file of Europarl data in French and to identify at most one fragment per sentence that would be a good candidate for revision and for which the annotator could think of reasonable paraphrases that did not involve changes to the envelope. Candidate fragments were accepted if they were not found in the French→English translation table. This step resulted in a corpus of 151 sentences with as many test fragments, with sizes ranging from 2 to 12 words, an average size of 5.38 words and a median size of 4 words.

Two native speakers, including the previous annotator, were asked to evaluate all paraphrased sentences on grammaticality and meaning. Contrary to previous works, we decided to use a smaller evaluation scale with only 3 values, as using more values tend to result in low inter-annotator agreement:

- 2: indicates that the paraphrase is perfect or almost perfect;
- 1: indicates that the paraphrase could become grammatical with one minor change, or that its meaning is almost clear;
- 0: indicates that more than one minor change is required to make the paraphrase grammatical or understandable.

### 4.3 Results and discussion

We ran both systems and took their one-best hypothesis for evaluation. Table 2 shows the results of a contrastive evaluation of the results obtained. For the 143 sentences for which paraphrases could be produced, we obtained 72 results common to both systems, and 71 which were specific to each system. The fact that for half of the cases the two systems produced the same paraphrases reveals that either context did not play an important role in these cases, and/or that the search space was rather limited due to the presence of rare words in the original fragment. Systems $S_{cont}$ and $S_{bas}$ are compared based on the number of cases were one was found to be better or worse than the other for the 71 cases where they proposed different paraphrases, either by the two judges (denoted by the $<$ and $>$ signs) or by one of the two judges while the other found the two systems to be of comparable performance (denoted by the $\leq$ and $\geq$ signs). As can be seen from the table, there is a clear preference for our $S_{cont}$ system, with a 31:37 ratio of cases where it is preferred for grammar, and 33:49 for meaning.

Table 3 shows absolute results for the same run of evaluation. First, it can be noted that both systems perform at a reasonable level, both for short and long text fragments. Several reasons may explain this: first, sentences to paraphrase are from the same domain as the training corpora for our SMT systems, which is a positive bias towards the paraphrasing systems. Also, the post-filtering heuristics and the fact that both systems could benefit from the knowledge of the target envelope during pivot-to-source back-translation certainly helped in filtering out incorrect paraphrases. These results confirm the trend observed on contrastive results that our $S_{cont}$ system is the best

[11]The unexpected worse performance of the fr→en system may be explained by issues related to tokenization after analysis by the parser.

[12]In our future work, we intend to investigate the possible use of lattices rather than $N$-best lists.

| | $S_{cont} < S_{bas}$ | $S_{cont} \leq S_{bas}$ | $S_{cont} \geq S_{bas}$ | $S_{cont} > S_{bas}$ | ? | Total |
|---|---|---|---|---|---|---|
| Grammar | 3 | 3 | 10 | 21 | 34 | 71 |
| Meaning | 3 | 13 | 13 | 20 | 22 | 71 |

Table 2: Contrastive results. The notation $S_{cont} < S_{bas}$ stands for cases in which $S_{cont}$ is found to be worse than $S_{bas}$ by both judges; $S_{cont} \leq S_{bas}$ for cases where $S_{cont}$ was found to be worse by one judge while the other found the two systems equivalent; similarly for other cases. '?' stands for cases where judges disagreed.

| | count | Grammar | | | Meaning | | | System | | |
|---|---|---|---|---|---|---|---|---|---|---|
| | | - | + | ? | - | + | ? | - | + | ? |
| $S_{bas}$ and $S_{cont}$ | 72 | 0 | 69 | 3 | 1 | 67 | 4 | 0 | 66 | 6 |
| $S_{bas}$ only | 71 | 13 | 46 | 12 | 18 | 41 | 12 | 9 | 39 | 23 |
| $S_{cont}$ only | 71 | 5 | 63 | 3 | 8 | 56 | 7 | 4 | 55 | 12 |
| $S_{bas}$: $2 \leq$ size $\leq 5$ | 81 | 6 | 69 | 6 | 10 | 63 | 8 | 4 | 61 | 16 |
| $S_{cont}$: $2 \leq$ size $\leq 5$ | 81 | 2 | 78 | 1 | 6 | 72 | 3 | 2 | 71 | 8 |
| $S_{bas}$: $6 \leq$ size $\leq 12$ | 62 | 7 | 46 | 9 | 9 | 45 | 8 | 5 | 44 | 13 |
| $S_{cont}$: $6 \leq$ size $\leq 12$ | 62 | 4 | 54 | 4 | 3 | 51 | 8 | 2 | 50 | 10 |

Table 3: Absolute results for manual evaluation. '+' indicates that both judges agree on a positive judgement (score 1 or 2), '-' that both judges agree on a negative judgment (score 0), and '?' that judges disagreed. 'System' judgments include judgments for both Grammar and Meaning.

performer for that task and that test set. It is however noteworthy that results were significantly better when they were produced by both systems, which may correspond to the easiest cases with respect to the training data and/or the task but also suggests the application of consensus techniques as done in MT system output combination.

Table 4 shows paraphrasing examples produced by $S_{cont}$. As can be noted from positive examples (a-c), the obtained paraphrases are mostly of the same syntactic types as the original phrases, which may be due to the proximity between the main language and the pivot language, as well as to the constraint on syntactic dependency preservation. Example (a) shows a case of what may be seen as some sort of normalization, as the concept of "*confidence of people*" (w.r.t. the English pivot language) may be more frequently expressed as *la confiance des citoyens (citizens)* than as *la confiance des gens (people)* in the reference corpus. Example (b), although showing a correct paraphrasing, contains an agreement error which is a result of the use of the gender neutral English pivot and the fact that the language model used by the pivot-to-source SMT system was not able to choose the correct agreement. Example (c) illustrates a case of correct paraphrasing involving reordering strongly influenced by the reordering required by the pivot language. The incorrect paraphrase of example (d) mainly results from the inability of the source-to-pivot SMT system to correctly translate the selected fragment; in particular, the syntactic structure was not correctly translated, and the noun *palier (stage)* was incorrectly translated as the verb *heal* and back-translated as the verb *traiter (heal, cure)*. Lastly, example (e) contains an error in word sense disambiguation between the pivot noun *act* and the noun *loi (law)*[13], as well as the incorrect deletion of the adverb *très fermement (firmly)* during source-to-pivot translation.

Several conclusions can be drawn from these results and observations. First, it is not surprising that the performance of the SMT systems used has an important impact on the results. This can be mitigated in several ways: by attempting paraphrasing on in-domain sentences; by using an appropriate pivot language with respect to the nature of the text fragment to paraphrase; by using one or several pivot languages (as proposed by (Bannard and Callison-Burch, 2005) for phrase paraphrasing) and consensus on the obtained paraphrases.

[13] This example might call for better lexical checking between original and paraphrased sentences, as well as exploiting context-aware SMT on the lower quality input of pivot-to-source translation.

| | |
|---|---|
| (a) | En tant que parti de gauche, nous avons dû, avec beaucoup de peine, nous rendre compte que les institutions ne sont pas des jeux de construction montables, transformables et démontables à souhait, mais qu'elles ont leur propre histoire et **doivent bénéficier de la confiance des gens** qui les soutiennent.<br>As the left, we have had, with a great deal of trouble, we see that the institutions are not games montables construction, transformables démontables and to wish, but they have their own history and **must enjoy the confidence of people** who support them.<br>→ **doivent avoir la confiance des citoyens** |
| (b) | Monsieur le président, **je suis inquiète au sujet de** l'attitude qui risque de se développer au sein de l'UE concernant la liberté des échanges.<br>Mr President, **I am concerned about** the attitude which might develop within the EU on free trade.<br>→ **je suis préoccupé par** |
| (c) | Ces accords constituent **un cadre contractuel entièrement nouveau** pour les pays de la région.<br>These agreements constitute **an entirely new contractual framework** for the countries of the region.<br>→ **un tout nouveau cadre contractuel** |
| (d) | Aujourd'hui, le durcissement parallèle des indépendantistes albanais et des autorités serbes **fait franchir à la crise un nouveau palier très inquiétant** dans la montée des tensions.<br>Today, the inflexibility parallel with the Albanian independent and the Serbian authorities **to overcome the crisis is a new heal very worrying** in the rise of tension.<br>→ (*) **de surmonter la crise est une nouvelle traiter très préoccupant** |
| (e) | La commission **condamne très fermement cet acte** et prend note de la décision de constituer un comité spécial au sein de la fiscalia general de la nación afin d'enquêter sur cet assassinat.<br>The Commission **condemn this act** and takes note of the decision to set up a special committee fiscalia within the general de la nacin in order to investigate this murder.<br>→ (*) **condamne cette loi** |

Table 4: Examples of sub-sentential paraphrasings produced by our $S_{cont}$ system.

Another remark is that our systems could be improved as regards their ability to exploit source context.[14]

## 5 Conclusion and future work

In this article, we have presented an approach to obtain sub-sentential paraphrases by using pivot SMT systems. Although our results showed that we were able to build a strong baseline on our test set, they also showed that integrating context both when translating from source-to-pivot and when back-translating from pivot-to-source can lead to improved performance. Our approach has the distinctive feature that it targets text fragments that can be larger than phrases traditionally captured by statistical techniques, while not targeting full sentences for which it would be harder to exploit context successfully. More generally, it addresses the case of the paraphrasing of text units for which no paraphrases are directly available.

We have identified several issues in our experiments that will constitute our future work. We intend to experiment with several pivot languages and to make them compete to obtain the $N$-best lists, as done in some approaches to multisource translation (Och and Ney, 2001) and/or to use a consensus technique to select the best paraphrase.

[14]It should be noted, however, that the reported experiments used relatively small amounts of training data as in most comparable works on context-aware Machine Translation.

As regards our context-aware SMT systems, we plan to exploit more complex syntactic knowledge and to learn correspondances for inter-fragment dependencies so as to make our rescoring based on syntactic dependencies more flexible. We are currently working on extracting revision instances from Wikipedia's revision history, which will provide us with a corpus of genuine revision occurrences as well as with an out-domain test corpus with reference paraphrases. Lastly, we want to investigate the use of our approach for two types of applications: text normalization, in which a text is revised to select approved phraseology and terminology, through the use of a carefully chosen training corpus for our pivot-to-source SMT system ; and interactive translation output revision for cases with or without a source text for professional translators or monolingual users.

## Acknowledgments

This work was funded by a grant from LIMSI.

## References

Salah Aït-Mokhtar, Jean-Pierre Chanod, and Claude Roux. 2002. Robustness beyond shallowness: incremental deep parsing. *Natural Language Engineering*, 8(3):121–144.

Colin Bannard and Chris Callison-Burch. 2005. Paraphrasing with bilingual parallel corpora. In *Proceedings of ACL*, Ann Arbor, USA.

Regina Barzilay and Lillian Lee. 2003. Learning to paraphrase: an unsupervised approach using multiple-sequence alignment. In *Proceedings of NAACL/HLT*, Edmonton, Canada.

Nicola Bertoldi, Madalina Barbaiani, Marcello Federico, and Roldano Cattoni. 2008. Phrase-based statistical machine translation with pivot languages. In *Proceeding of IWSLT*, pages 143–149, Hawaii, USA.

Rahul Bhagat and Deepak Ravichandran. 2008. Large scale acquisition of paraphrases for learning surface patterns. In *Proceedings of ACL: HLT*, Columbus, USA.

Chris Callison-Burch, Trevor Cohn, and Mirella Lapata. 2008. Parametric: An automatic evaluation metric for paraphrasing. In *Proceedings of COLING*, Manchester, UK.

Chris Callison-Burch. 2008. Syntactic constraints on paraphrases extracted from parallel corpora. In *Proceedings of EMNLP*, Hawai, USA.

Marine Carpuat and Dekai Wu. 2007. Context-dependent phrasal translation lexicons for statistical machine translation. In *Proceedings of Machine Translation Summit XI*, Copenhagen, Denmark.

Michael Connor and Dan Roth. 2007. Context sensitive paraphrasing with a single unsupervised classifier. In *Proceedings of ECML*, Warsaw, Poland.

Walter Daelemans, Jakub Zavrel, Ko van der Sloot, and Antal van den Bosch. 2007. TiMBL: Tilburg Memory Based Learner, version 6.1, Reference Guide. Technical report, ILK 07-xx. Available from `http://ilk.uvt.nl/downloads/pub/papers/ilk0703.pdf`.

Bill Dolan, Chris Quirk, and Chris Brockett. 2004. Unsupervised construction of large paraphrase corpora: Exploiting massively parallel news sources. In *Proceedings of Coling 2004*, pages 350–356, Geneva, Switzerland.

Kevin Gimpel and Noah A. Smith. 2008. Rich source-side context for statistical machine translation. In *Proceedings of WMT at ACL*, Columbus, USA.

Rejwanul Haque, Sudip Kumar Naskar, Yanjun Ma, and Andy Way. 2009. Using supertags as source language context in smt. In *Proceedings of EAMT*, Barcelona, Spain.

Philipp Koehn, Hieu Hoang, Alexandra Birch, Chris Callison-Burch, Marcello Federico, Nicola Bertoldi, Brooke Cowan, Wade Shen, Christine Moran, Richard Zens, Chris Dyer, Ondrej Bojar, Alexandra Constantin, and Evan Herbst. 2007. Moses: Open source toolkit for statistical machine translation. In *Proceedings of ACL, demo session*, Prague, Czech Republic.

Philipp Koehn. 2005. Europarl: A parallel corpus for statistical machine translation. In *Proceedings of MT Summit*, Phuket, Thailand.

Nitin Madnani, Necip Fazil Ayan, Philip Resnik, and Bonnie J. Dorr. 2007. Paraphrases for parameter tuning in statistical machine translation. In *Proceedings of Workshop on Machine Translation at ACL*, Prague, Czech Republic.

Aurélien Max, Rafik Makhloufi, and Philippe Langlais. 2008. Explorations in using grammatical dependencies for contextual phrase translation disambiguation. In *Proceedings of EAMT*, Hamburg, Germany.

Aurélien Max. 2008. Local rephrasing suggestions for supporting the work of writers. In *Proceedings of GoTAL*, Gothenburg, Sweden.

Rani Nelken and Elif Yamangil. 2008. Mining wikipedia's article revision history for training computational linguistics algorithms. In *Proceedings of the AAAI Workshop on Wikipedia and Artificial Intelligence: An Evolving Synergy*, Chicago, USA.

Franz Josef Och and Hermann Ney. 2001. Statistical multi-source translation. In *Proceedings of MT Summit*, Santiago de Compostela, Spain.

Bo Pang, Kevin Knight, and Daniel Marcu. 2003. Syntax-based alignment of multiple translations: Extracting paraphrases and generating new sentences. In *Proceedings of NAACL/HLT*, Edmonton, Canada.

Chris Quirk, Chris Brockett, and William B. Dolan. 2004. Monolingual machine translation for paraphrase generation. In *Proceedings of EMNLP*, Barcelona, Spain.

Nicolas Stroppa, Antal van den Bosch, and Andy Way. 2007. Exploiting source similarity for smt using context-informed features. In *Proceedings of TMI*, Skvde, Sweden.

Hua Wu and Haifeng Wang. 2007. Pivot language approach for phrase-based statistical machine translation. In *Proceedings of the 45th Annual Meeting of the Association of Computational Linguistics*, Prague, Czech Republic.

Shiqi Zhao, Cheng Niu, Ming Zhou, and Sheng Li. 2008a. Combining multiple resources to improve smt-based paraphrasing model. In *Proceedings of ACL-HLT*, Columbus, USA.

Shiqi Zhao, Haifeng Wang, Ting Liu, and Sheng Li. 2008b. Pivot approach for extracting paraphrase patterns from bilingual corpora. In *Proceedings of ACL-HLT*, Columbus, USA.

# Augmenting WordNet-based Inference with Argument Mapping

**Idan Szpektor**
Department of Computer Science
Bar-Ilan University
Ramat Gan, Israel
szpekti@cs.biu.ac.il

**Ido Dagan**
Department of Computer Science
Bar-Ilan University
Ramat Gan, Israel
dagan@cs.biu.ac.il

## Abstract

WordNet is a useful resource for lexical inference in applications. Inference over predicates, however, often requires a change in argument positions, which is not specified in WordNet. We propose a novel framework for augmenting WordNet-based inferences over predicates with corresponding argument mappings. We further present a concrete implementation of this framework, which yields substantial improvement to WordNet-based inference.

## 1 Introduction

WordNet (Miller, 1995), a manually constructed lexical database, is probably the mostly used resource for lexical inference in NLP tasks, such as Question Answering (QA), Information Extraction (IE), Information Retrieval and Textual Entailment (RTE) (Moldovan and Mihalcea, 2000; Pasca and Harabagiu, 2001; Bar-Haim et al., 2006; Giampiccolo et al., 2007).

Inference using WordNet typically involves lexical substitutions for words in text based on WordNet relations, a process known as lexical chains (Barzilay and Elhadad, 1997; Moldovan and Novischi, 2002). For example, the answer to "*From which country was Louisiana acquired?*" can be inferred from "*The United States bought up Louisiana from France*" using the chains 'France ⇒ European country ⇒ country' and 'buy up ⇒ buy ⇒ acquire'.

When performing inference between predicates there is an additional complexity on top of lexical substitution: the syntactic relationship between the predicate and its arguments may change as well. For example, '$X$ buy $Y$ for $Z$ ⇒ $X$ pay $Z$ for $Y$'.

Currently, argument mappings are not specified for WordNet's relations. Therefore, correct WordNet inference chains over predicates can be performed only for substitution relations (mainly synonyms and hypernyms, e.g. 'buy ⇒ acquire'), for which argument positions do not change. Other relation types that may be used for inference cannot be utilized when the predicate arguments need to be traced as well. Examples include the WordNet 'entailment' relation (e.g. 'buy ⇒ pay') and relations between morphologically derived words (e.g. 'acquire ⇔ acquisition').

Our goal is to obtain argument mappings for WordNet relations that are often used for inference. In this paper we address several prominent WordNet relations, including verb-noun derivations and the verb-verb 'entailment' and 'cause' relations, referred henceforth as *inferential relations*. Under the Textual Entailment paradigm, all these relations can be viewed as expressing entailment. Accordingly, we propose a novel framework, called *Argument-mapped WordNet (AmWN)*, that represents argument mappings for inferential relations as entailment rules. These rules are augmented with subcategorization frames and functional roles, which are proposed as a generally-needed extension for predicative entailment rules.

Following our new representation scheme, we present a concrete implementation of AmWN for a large number of WordNet's relations. The mappings for these relations are populated by combining information from manual and corpus-based resources, which provides broader coverage compared to prior work and more accurate mappings. Table 1 shows typical inference chains obtained



*Proceedings of the 2009 Workshop on Applied Textual Inference, ACL-IJCNLP 2009*, pages 27–35,
Suntec, Singapore, 6 August 2009. 

| Rule Chains |
|---|
| shopping:n of $X_{obj}$ $\Rightarrow$ buying:n of $X_{obj}$ $\Rightarrow$ buy:v $X_{obj}$ $\Rightarrow$ pay:v for $X_{mod}$ |
| vote:v on $X_{mod}$ $\Rightarrow$ decide:v on $X_{mod}$ $\Rightarrow$ debate:v $X_{obj}$ |
| $X_{obj}$'s sentence:n $\Rightarrow$ condemn:v $X_{obj}$ $\Rightarrow$ convict:v $X_{obj}$ $\Rightarrow$ $X_{obj}$'s conviction:n |
| $X_{ind-obj}$'s teacher:n $\Rightarrow$ teach:v to $X_{ind-obj}$ $\Rightarrow$ $X_{subj}$ learn:v |

Table 1: Examples for inference chains obtained using AmWN. Arguments are subscripted with functional roles, e.g. subject (subj) and indirect-object (ind-obj). For brevity, predicate frames are omitted.

using our implementation.

To further improve WordNet-based inference for NLP applications, we address the phenomena of rare WordNet senses. Rules generated for such senses might hurt inference accuracy since they are often applied incorrectly to texts when matched against inappropriate, but more frequent senses of the rule words. Since word sense disambiguation (WSD) solutions are typically not sufficiently robust yet, most applications do not currently apply WSD methods. Hence, we propose to optionally filter out such rules using a novel corpus-based validation algorithm.

We tested both WordNet and AmWN on a test set derived from a standard IE benchmark. The results show that AmWN substantially improves WordNet-based inference in terms of both recall and precision[1].

## 2 Argument-Mapping Entailment Rules

In our framework we represent argument mappings for inferential relations between predicates through an extension of entailment rules over syntactic representations. As defined in earlier works, an *entailment rule* specifies an inference relation between an entailing template and an entailed template, where *templates* are parse subtrees with argument variables (Szpektor and Dagan, 2008). For example, '$X \xleftarrow{subj}$ buy $\xrightarrow{obj} Y$ $\Rightarrow$ '$X \xleftarrow{subj}$ pay $\xrightarrow{prep-for} Y$'.

When a rule is applied to a text, a new consequent is inferred by instantiating the entailed template variables with the argument instantiations of the entailing template in the text. In our example, "*IBM paid for Cognos*" can be inferred from "*IBM bought Cognos*". This way, the syntactic structure of the rule templates specifies the required argument positions for correct argument mapping.

However, representing entailment rule structure only by syntactic argument positions is insufficient for predicative rules. Correct argument mapping depends also on the specific *syntactic functional roles* of the arguments (subject, object etc.) and on the suitable *subcategorization frame* (*frame*) for the predicate mention - a set of functional roles that a predicate may occur with. For example, '$X$'s buyout $\Rightarrow$ buy $X$' is incorrectly applied to "*IBM's buyout of Cognos*" if roles are ignored, since 'IBM' plays the subject role while $X$ needs to be an object.

Seeking to address this issue, we were inspired by the Nomlex database (Macleod et al., 1998) (see Section 3.2.1) and explicitly specify argument mapping for each frame and functional role. As in Nomlex, we avoid the use of semantic roles and stick to the syntactic level, augmenting the representation of templates with: (a) a syntactic functional role for each argument; (b) the valid predicate frame for this template mentions. We note that such functional roles typically coincide with dependency relations of the verbal form. A rule example is '$X_{subj}$ $\text{break}_{\{intrans\}}$ $\Rightarrow$ $\text{damage}_{\{trans\}}$ $X_{obj}$'[2]. More examples are shown in Table 1.

Unlike Nomlex records, our templates can be partial: they may contain only some of the possible predicate arguments, e.g. '$\text{buy}_{\{trans\}}$ $X_{obj}$', where the subject, included in the frame, is omitted. Partial templates are necessary for matching predicate occurrences that include only some of the possible arguments, as in "*Cognos was bought yesterday*". Additionally, some resources, such as automatic rule learning methods (Lin and Pantel, 2001; Sekine, 2005), can provide only partial argument information, and we would want to represent such knowledge as well.

In our framework we follow (Szpektor and Dagan, 2008) and use only rules between *unary templates*, containing a single argument. Such templates can describe any argument mapping by de-

[1]We plan to make our AmWN publicly available.

[2]Functional roles are denoted by subscripts of the arguments and frames by subscripts of the predicate. We shorthand *trans* for transitive frame {*subject*, *object*} and *intrans* for intransitive {*subject*}. For brevity, we will not show all template information when examples are self explanatory.

composing templates with several arguments into unary ones, while preserving the specification of the subcategorization frame.

To apply a rule, the entailing template must be first matched in the text, which includes matching the template's syntactic dependency structure, functional roles, and frame. Such procedure requires texts to be annotated with these types of information. This can be reasonably performed with existing tools and resources, as described for our own text processing in Section 4.

Explicitly matching frames and functional roles in rules avoids incorrect rule applications. For example, '$X_{obj}$'s buyout $\Rightarrow$ buy $X_{obj}$' would be applied only to "*Cognos's buyout by IBM*" following proper role annotation of the text, but not to "*IBM's buyout of Cognos*". As another example, '$X_{subj}$ break$_{\{intrans\}}$ $\Rightarrow$ damage$_{\{trans\}}$ $X_{obj}$' would be applied only to the intransitive occurrence of 'break', e.g. "*The vase broke*", but not to "*John broke the vase*".

Ambiguous cases may occur during annotation. For example, the role of 'John' in "*John's invitation was well intended*" could be either subject or object. Such recognized ambiguities should be left unannotated, blocking incorrect rule application.

## 3 Argument Mapping for WordNet

Following our extension of entailment rules, we present *Argument-mapped WordNet* (*AmWN*), a framework for extending WordNet's inferential relations with argument mapping at the syntactic representation level.

### 3.1 Argument Mapping Representation

The AmWN structure follows that of WordNet: a directed graph whose nodes are WordNet synsets and edges are relations between synsets. Since we focus on entailment between predicates, we include only predicative synsets: all verb synsets and noun synsets identified as predicates (see Section 3.2). In addition, only WordNet relations that correspond to some type of entailment are considered, as detailed in Section 3.2.

In our framework, different subcategorization frames are treated as having different "meanings", since different frames may correspond to different entailment rules. Each WordNet synset is split into several nodes, one for each of its frames. We take frame descriptions for verbs from WordNet[3].

[3]We also tried using VerbNet (Kipper et al., 2000), without any current performance improvement.

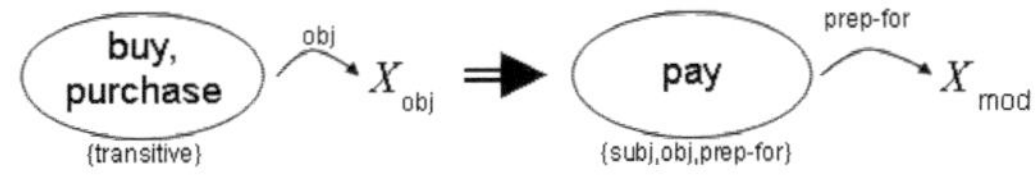


Figure 1: A description of 'buy/purchase $X \Rightarrow$ pay for $X$' as a mapping edge in AmWN.

Since WordNet does not provide frames for noun predicates, these are taken from Nomlex-plus (see Section 3.2).

There are two types of graph edges that represent entailment rules between nodes: mapping edges and substitution edges. Mapping edges specify entailment rules that require argument mapping, where the entailing and entailed template predicates are replaced by synsets. Thus, an edge represents all rules between entailing and entailed synset members, as in Figure 1.

Substitution edges connect pairs of predicates, of the same part-of-speech, which preserve argument positions in inference. This is analogous to how WordNet may be currently used for inference via the *synonym* and *hypernym* relations. Unlike WordNet, substitution edges in AmWN may connect only nodes that have the same subcategorization frame.

AmWN is utilized by generating rule chains for a given input unary template. First, starting nodes that match the input predicate are selected. Then, rules are generated by traversing either incoming or outgoing graph edges transitively, depending on the entailment direction requested. Specific synset-ids, if known, may also be added to the input to constrain the relevant starting nodes for the input predicate. Table 1 shows examples of rule chains from AmWN.

### 3.2 Argument Mapping Population

After defining the AmWN representation, we next describe our implementation of AmWN. We first populate the AmWN graph with substitution edges for WordNet's hypernyms and synonyms (as self edges), e.g. 'buy $\Leftrightarrow$ purchase' and 'buy $\Rightarrow$ acquire'. The following subsections describe how mapping edges are created based on various manual and corpus-based information resources.

#### 3.2.1 Nominalization Relations

The relation between a verb and its nominalizations, e.g. between 'employ' and 'employment',

```
:ORTH "employment"
:VERB "employ"
:VERB-SUBC ((NOM-NP
             :SUBJECT ((DET-POSS)
                       (N-N-MOD)
                       (PP :PVAL ("by")))
             :OBJECT ((DET-POSS)
                      (PP :PVAL ("of")))
```

Figure 2: Part of the *employment* Nomlex entry, describing the possible syntactic dependency positions for each role of the transitive frame. It states, for example, that the verbal 'object' role can be mapped to *employment* either as a possessive or as the complement of the preposition 'of'.

is described in WordNet by the *derivationally related* relation. To add argument mappings for these relations we utilize Nomlex-plus (Meyers et al., 2004), a database of around 5000 English nominalizations. Nomlex specifies for each verbal subcategorization frame of each nominalization how its argument positions are mapped to functional roles of related verbs.

For each Nomlex entry, we extract all possible argument mappings between the verbal and nominal forms, as well as between different argument realizations of the noun. For example, the mappings '$X_{obj}$'s employment ⇔ employ $X_{obj}$' and '$X_{obj}$'s employment ⇔ employment of $X_{obj}$' are derived from the entry in Figure 2.

The major challenge in integrating Nomlex and WordNet is to identify for each Nomlex noun which WordNet synsets describe its predicative meanings. For example, one synset of 'acquisition' that is derivationally related to 'acquire' is not predicative: "*an ability that has been acquired by training*". We mark noun synsets as predicative if they are (transitive) hyponyms of the *act* high-level synset.

Once predicative synsets are identified, we create, for each synset, a node for each subcategorization frame of its noun members, as found in Nomlex-plus. In some nodes not all original synset members are retained, since not all members share all their frames. Mapping edges are then added between nodes that have the same frame. We add both noun-verb edges and noun self-edges that map different realizations of the same functional role (e.g. '$X_{obj}$'s employment ⇔ employment of $X_{obj}$').

As rich as Nomlex-plus is, it still does not include all nominalizations. For example, the nouns

| Lexical Relation | Extracted Mappings |
|---|---|
| buy ⇒ pay | buy for $X$ ⇒ pay $X$<br>$X$ buy ⇒ $X$ pay |
| divorce ⇒ marry | divorce from $X$ ⇒ marry $X$<br>divorce from $X$ ⇒ $X$ marry |
| kill ⇒ die | kill $X$ ⇒ $X$ die<br>kill among $X$ ⇒ $X$ die |
| breathe ⇒ inhale | breathe $X$ ⇒ inhale $X$<br>breathe in $X$ ⇒ inhale $X$ |
| remind ⇒ remember | remind $X$ ⇒ $X$ remember<br>remind of $X$ ⇒ remember $X$ |
| teach ⇒ learn | teach $X$ ⇒ learn $X$<br>teach to $X$ ⇒ $X$ learn |
| give ⇒ have | give $X$ ⇒ have $X$<br>give to $X$ ⇒ $X$ have |

Table 2: Some argument mappings for WordNet verb-verb relations discovered by unary-DIRT.

'divorce' (related to the verb 'divorce') and 'striking' are missing. WordNet has a much richer set of nominalizations that we would like to use. To do so, we inherit associated frames and argument realizations for each nominalization synset from its closest hypernym that does appear in Nomlex. Thus, 'divorce' inherits its information from 'separation' and 'striking' inherits from 'hit'. A by-product of this process is the automatic extension of Nomlex-plus with 5100 new nominalization entries, based on the inherited information[4].

### 3.2.2 Verb-Verb Relations

There are two inferential relations between verbs in WordNet that do not preserve argument positions: *cause* and *entailment*. Unlike for nominalizations, there is no broad-coverage manual resource of argument mapping for these relations. Hence, we turn to unsupervised approaches that learn entailment rules from corpus statistics.

Many algorithms were proposed for learning entailment rules between templates from corpora (Lin and Pantel, 2001; Szpektor et al., 2004; Sekine, 2005), but typically with mediocre accuracy. However, we only search for rules between verbs for which WordNet already indicates the existence of an entailment relation and are thus not affected by rules that wrongly relate non-entailing verbs. We acquired a rule-set containing the top 300 rules for every unary template in the Reuters RCV1 corpus[5] by implementing the unary-DIRT algorithm (Szpektor and Dagan, 2008), which was shown to have relatively high recall compared to other algorithms.

[4]We plan making this extension publicly available as well.
[5]http://about.reuters.com/researchandstandards/corpus/

To extract argument mappings, we identify all AmWN node pairs whose synsets are related in WordNet by a *cause* or an *entailment* relation. For each pair, we look for unary-DIRT rules between any pair of members in the entailing and entailed synsets. For example, the synset {buy, purchase} entails {pay}, so we look for rules mapping either 'buy ⇒ pay' or 'purchase ⇒ pay'. Table 2 presents examples for discovered mappings. While unary-DIRT rules are not annotated with functional roles, they can be derived straightforwardly from the verbal dependency relations available in the rule's templates. The obtained rules are then added to AmWN as mapping edges.

We only search for rules that map a functional role in the frame of one verb to any role for the other verb. Focusing on frame elements avoids extracting mapping rules learned for adjuncts, which tend to be of low precision.

### 3.3 Rule Filtering

In preliminary analysis we found two phenomena, *sense drifting* and *rare senses*, which may reduce the effectiveness of AmWN-based inference even if each graph edge by itself, taken out of context, is correct. To address these phenomena within practical inference we propose the following optional methods for rule filtering.

**Sense Drifting** WordNet verbs typically have a more fine-grained set of synsets than their related nominalizations. There are cases where several verb synsets are related to the same nominal synset. Since entailment between a verb and its nominalization is bidirectional, all such verb synsets would end up entailing each other via the nominal node.

Alas, some of these connected verb synsets represent quite different meanings, which results in incorrect inferences. This problem, which we call *sense drifting*, is demonstrated in Figure 3. To address it, we constrain each rule generation chain to include at most one verb-noun edge, which still connects the noun and verb hierarchies.

**Rare Senses** Some word senses in WordNet are rare. Thus, applying rules that correspond to such senses yields many incorrect inferences, since they are typically matched against other frequent senses of the word. Such a rule is 'have $X \Rightarrow X$ is born', corresponding to a rare sense of 'have'. WSD is a possible solution for this problem. However, most state-of-the-art IE, QA and RTE systems do not rely on WSD methods, which are currently not sufficiently robust.

To circumvent the rare sense problem, we instead filter out such rules. Each AmWN rule is validated against our unary-DIRT rule-set, which, being corpus-based, contains mostly rules for frequent senses. A rule is *directly-validated* if it is in the corpus-based rule-set, or if it is a nominal-verb rule which describes a reliable morphological change for a predicate. The AmWN graph-path that generated each rule is automatically examined. A rule is considered *valid* if there is a sequence of directly-validated intermediate rules along the path whose transitive chaining generates the rule. Invalid rules are filtered out.

To illustrate, suppose the rule 'a ⇒ d' was generated by the chain 'a ⇒ b ⇒ c ⇒ d'. It is valid if there is a rule chain along the path that yields 'a ⇒ d', e.g. {'a ⇒ b','b ⇒ c','c ⇒ d'} or {'a ⇒ b', 'b ⇒ d'}, whose rules are all directly-validated.

## 4 Experimental Setup

We follow here the experimental setup presented in (Szpektor and Dagan, 2008), testing the generated rules on the ACE 2005 event dataset[6]. This standard IE benchmark includes 33 types of event predicates such as *Injure, Sue* and *Divorce*[7]. The ACE guidelines specify for each event its possible arguments. For example, some of the *Injure* event arguments are *Agent* and *Victim*. All event mentions, including their instantiated arguments, are annotated in a corpus collected from various sources (newswire articles, blogs, etc.).

To utilize the ACE dataset for evaluating rule applications, each ACE event predicate was represented by a set of unary *seed templates*, one for each event argument. Example seed templates for *Injure* are '$A$ injure' and 'injure $V$'. Each event argument is mapped to the corresponding seed template variable, e.g. '*Agent*' to $A$ and '*Victim*' to $V$ in the above example.

We manually annotated each seed template with a subcategorization frame and an argument functional role, e.g. 'injure$_{\{trans\}}$ $V_{obj}$'. We also included relevant WordNet synset-ids, so only rules fitting the target meaning of the event will be extracted. In this experiment, we focused only on the core semantic arguments. Adjuncts (time and

[6]http://projects.ldc.upenn.edu/ace/

[7]Only 26 frequent event types that correspond to a unique predicate were tested, following (Szpektor and Dagan, 2008).

| | Synset Members | WordNet Gloss |
|---|---|---|
| (verb) | collar, nail, apprehend, **arrest**, pick up, nab, cop | take into custody |
| ⇕ | | |
| (noun) | apprehension, arrest, catch, collar, pinch, taking into custody | the act of apprehending (especially apprehending a criminal) |
| ⇕ | | |
| (verb) | get, catch, capture | succeed in catching or seizing, especially after a chase |
| ⇕ | | |
| (noun) | capture, seizure | the act of taking of a person by force |
| ⇕ | | |
| (verb) | seize | take or capture by force |
| ⇑ (hypernym) | | |
| (verb) | **kidnap**, nobble, abduct, snatch | take away to an undisclosed location against their will and usually in order to extract a ransom |

Figure 3: A WordNet sense-drifting traversal, generating the incorrect inference 'kidnap $\Rightarrow$ arrest'.

place) were ignored since they typically don't require argument mapping, the main target for our assessment.

The ACE corpus was dependency-parsed with Minipar (Lin, 1998) and annotated with functional roles and frames for each predicate mention. The functional roles for a verb mention were taken directly from the corresponding dependency tree relations. Its frame was chosen to be the largest WordNet frame of that verb that matched the mention's roles.

Nominalization frames and functional roles in the text were annotated using our extended Nomlex-plus database. For each nominal mention, we found the largest Nomlex frame whose syntactic argument positions matched those of the mention's arguments. The arguments were then annotated with the specified roles of the chosen frame. Ambiguous cases, where the same argument position could match multiple roles, were left unannotated, as discussed in Section 2.

Argument mentions for events were found in the annotated corpus by matching either the seed templates or the templates entailing them in some rules. The matching procedure follows the one described in Section 2. Templates are matched using a syntactic matcher that handles simple syntactic variations such as passive-form and conjunctions. For example, 'wound$_{\{trans\}}$ $V_{obj}$ $\Rightarrow$ injure$_{\{trans\}}$ $V_{obj}$' was matched in the text "Hagel$_{obj}$ *was* wounded$_{trans}$ *in Vietnam*". A rule application is considered correct if the matched argument is annotated in the corpus with the corresponding ACE role.

We note that our system performance on the ACE task as such is limited. First, WordNet does not provide all types of needed rules. Second, the system of our experimental setting is rather basic, with limited matching capabilities and without a WSD module. However, this test-set is still very useful for relative comparison of WordNet and our proposed AmWN.

## 5 Results and Analysis

We tested four different rule-set configurations: a) only the seed templates, without any rules; b) rules generated based on WordNet 3.0 without argument mapping, using only synonym and hypernym relations; c) WordNet rules from (b), filtered using our corpus-based validation method for rare senses; d) rules generated from our AmWN.

Out of the 8953 non-substitutable inferential relations that we identified in WordNet, our AmWN implementation created mapping edges for 75% of 8325 Noun-Verb relations and 70% of 628 Verb-Verb relations. Altogether 41549 mapping edges between synset nodes were added. A manual error analysis of these mappings is provided in Section 5.2.

Each configuration was evaluated for each ACE event. We measured the percentage of correct argument mentions extracted out of all correct argument mentions annotated for the event (recall) and out of all argument mentions extracted (precision), and F1, their harmonic average. We report macro averages over the 26 event types.

### 5.1 Results

Table 3 summarizes the results for the different configurations. As expected, matching only the seed templates yields the highest precision but lowest recall. Using the standard WordNet configuration actually decreases overall F1 performance. Though recall increases relatively by 30%, thanks to WordNet expansions, F1 is penalized by a sharp

| Configuration | R (%) | P (%) | F1 |
|---|---|---|---|
| No Rules | 13.5 | 63.0 | 20.7 |
| WordNet | 17.5 | 35.3 | 18.5 |
| WordNet with rule validation | 16.5 | 46.9 | 20.4 |
| AmWN | 20.8 | 43.9 | 24.2 |

Table 3: Recall (R), Precision (P) and F1 results for the different tested configurations.

relative drop in precision (by 56%). The main reason for this decline is the application of rules involving infrequent word senses, as elaborated in Section 3.3.

When our rule validation approach is applied to standard WordNet expansions, a much higher precision is achieved with only a small decline in recall. This shows that our corpus-based filtering method manages to avoid many of the noisy rules for rare senses, while maintaining those that are frequently involved in inference.

Finally, our main result shows that adding argument mapping improves performance substantially. AmWN achieves a much higher recall than WordNet. Recall increases relatively by 26% over validated WordNet, and by 54% over the no-rules baseline. Furthermore, precision drops only slightly, by 6%, compared to validated WordNet. This shows that argument mapping increases WordNet's graph connectivity, while our rule-validation method maintains almost the same precision for many more generated rules. The improvement in overall F1 performance is statistically significant compared to all other configurations, according to the two-sided Wilcoxon signed rank test at the level of 0.01 (Wilcoxon, 1945).

### 5.2 Error Analysis

We manually analyzed the reasons for false positives (incorrect extractions) and false negatives (missed extractions) of AmWN by sampling 300 extractions of each type.

From the false positives analysis (Table 4) we see that practically all generated rules are correct (99.4%), that is, they would be valid in some contexts. Almost all errors come from matching errors (including parse errors) and context mismatches, due to our limited IE implementation. The only two incorrect rules sampled were due to an incorrect Nomlex entry and a WordNet synset that should have been split into two separate senses. Considering that correct extractions resulted, per our analysis, from correct rules, the analysis of this sample indicates that virtually all AmWN edges that get utilized in practice are correct.

| Reason | % mentions |
|---|---|
| Context mismatch | 57.2 |
| Match error | 33.6 |
| Errors in gold-standard annotation | 8.6 |
| Incorrect Rule learned | 0.6 |

Table 4: Distribution of reasons for false positives (incorrect argument extractions).

| Reason | % mentions |
|---|---|
| Rule not learned | 67.7 |
| Match error | 18.0 |
| Discourse analysis needed | 12.0 |
| Argument is predicative | 1.3 |
| Errors in gold-standard annotation | 1.0 |

Table 5: Distribution of reasons for false negatives (missed argument mentions).

Context mismatches, which constitute the majority of errors (57.2%), occur when the entailing template of a rule is matched in inappropriate contexts. This occurs typically when the match is against another sense of the predicate, or when an argument is not of the requested type (e.g. "*The Enron sentence*" vs. "*A one month sentence*"). In future work, we plan to address this problem by utilizing context-sensitive application of rules in the spirit of (Szpektor et al., 2008).

Table 5 presents the false negatives analysis. Most missed extractions are due to rules that were not learned (67.7%). These mainly involve complex templates ('file a lawsuit ⇔ sue') and inference rules that are not synonyms/hypernyms ('execute ⇒ sentence'), which are not widely annotated in WordNet. From further analysis, we found that 10% of these misses are due to rules that are generated from AmWN but filtered out by one of our filtering methods (Section 3.3).

12% of the arguments cannot be extracted by rules alone, due to required discourse analysis, while 18% of the mentions were missed due to incorrect syntactic matching. By assuming correct matches in these cases and avoiding rule filtering, we can estimate the upper bound recall of the rule-set for the ACE dataset to be 40%.

In conclusion, for better performance the system should be augmented with context modeling and better template matching. Additionally, other rule-bases, e.g. DIRT (Lin and Pantel, 2001), should be added to increase rule coverage.

| Configuration | R (%) | P (%) | F1 |
|---|---|---|---|
| AmWN | 20.8 | 43.9 | 24.2 |
| No nominalization mappings | 18.1 | 45.5 | 21.8 |
| No verb-verb mappings | 19.3 | 43.8 | 22.8 |
| No rule validation | 22.0 | 30.4 | 20.9 |
| No sense drift blocking | 22.5 | 37.4 | 21.7 |

Table 6: The Recall (R), Precision (P) and F1 results for ablation tests.

### 5.3 Component Analysis

Table 6 presents ablations tests that assess the marginal contribution of each AmWN component. Nominal-verb and verb-verb mappings contribute to the graph connectivity, hence the recall reduction when they are removed.

Complementary to recall components, rule filtering improves precision. When removing the corpus-based rule-validation, recall increases relatively by 6% but precision drops relatively by 30%, showing the benefit of noisy-rule filtering. Allowing sense drifting hurts precision, a relative drop of 22%. Yet, recall increases relatively by 8%, indicating that some verb synsets, connected via a shared nominal, entail each other even though they are not connected directly. For example, 'found $X \Leftrightarrow$ create $X$' was generated only via the shared nominal 'founding'. In future work, we plan to apply AmWN to a coarse-grained set of WordNet synsets (Palmer et al., 2007) as a possible solution to sense drifting.

## 6 Related Work

Several works attempt to extend WordNet with additional lexical semantic information (Moldovan and Rus, 2001; Snow et al., 2006; Suchanek et al., 2007; Clark et al., 2008). However, the only previous work we are aware of that enriches WordNet with argument mappings is (Novischi and Moldovan, 2006). This work utilizes VerbNet's subcategorization frames to identify possible verb arguments. Argument mapping is provided only between verbs, ignoring relations between verbs and nouns. Arguments are mapped based on thematic role names shared between frames of different verbs. However, the semantic interpretation of thematic roles is generally inconsistent across verbs (Lowe et al., 1997; Kaisser and Webber, 2007). Instead, we discover these mappings from corpus statistics, offering an accurate approach (as analyzed in Section 5.2).

A frame semantics approach for argument mapping between predicates is proposed by the FrameNet project (Baker et al., 1998). Currently, FrameNet is the only resource for frame-semantic argument mappings. However, it is manually constructed and currently covers much less predicates and relations than WordNet. Furthermore, frame-semantic parsers are less robust than syntactic parsers, presently hindering the utilization of this approach in applications (Burchardt and Pennacchiotti, 2008).

Nomlex argument mapping patterns similar to ours were derived for IE in (Meyers et al., 1998), but they were not integrated with any additional information, such as WordNet.

## 7 Conclusions

We presented Argument-mapped WordNet (AmWN), a novel framework for augmenting WordNet with argument mappings at the syntactic representation level. With AmWN, non-substitutable WordNet relations can also be utilized correctly, increasing the coverage of WordNet-based inference. The standard entailment rule representation is augmented in our work with functional roles and subcategorization frames, shown to be a feasible extension needed for correct rule application in general.

Our implementation of AmWN populates WordNet with mappings based on combining manual and corpus-based resources. It covers a broader range of relations compared to prior work and yields more accurate mappings. We also introduced a novel corpus-based validation mechanism, avoiding rules for infrequent senses. Our experiments show that AmWN substantially improves standard WordNet-based inference.

In future work we plan to add mappings between verbs and adjectives and between different frames of a verb. We also want to incorporate resources for additional subcategorization frames, such as VerbNet. Finally, we plan to enhance our text annotation based on noun-compound disambiguation (Lapata and Lascarides, 2003).


## Acknowledgements

This work was partially supported by the NEGEV project (www.negev-initiative.org), the PASCAL-2 Network of Excellence of the European Community FP7-ICT-2007-1-216886, the FBK-irst/Bar-Ilan University collaboration and the Israel Science Foundation grant 1112/08.

## References


Collin F. Baker, Charles J. Fillmore, and John B. Lowe. 1998. The berkeley framenet project. In *Proceedings of ACL.*

Roy Bar-Haim, Ido Dagan, Bill Dolan, Lisa Ferro, Danilo Giampiccolo, Bernardo Magnini, and Idan Szpektor. 2006. The second pascal recognising textual entailment challenge. In *Second PASCAL Challenge Workshop for Recognizing Textual Entailment.*

Regina Barzilay and Michael Elhadad. 1997. Using lexical chains for text summarization. In *Proceedings of ACL.*

Aljoscha Burchardt and Marco Pennacchiotti. 2008. Fate: a framenet-annotated corpus for textual entailment. In *Proceedings of LREC.*

Peter Clark, Christiane Fellbaum, Jerry R. Hobbs, Phil Harrison, William R. Murray, and John Thompson. 2008. Augmenting WordNet for Deep Understanding of Text. In *Proceedings of STEP 2008.*

Danilo Giampiccolo, Bernardo Magnini, Ido Dagan, and Bill Dolan. 2007. The third pascal recognizing textual entailment challenge. In *Proceedings of the ACL-PASCAL Workshop on Textual Entailment and Paraphrasing.*

Michael Kaisser and Bonnie Webber. 2007. Question answering based on semantic roles. In *ACL 2007 Workshop on Deep Linguistic Processing.*

Karin Kipper, Hoa Trang Dang, and Martha Palmer. 2000. Class-based construction of a verb lexicon. In *Proceedings of AAAI.*

Mirella Lapata and Alex Lascarides. 2003. Detecting novel compounds: The role of distributional evidence. In *Proceedings of EACL.*

Dekang Lin and Patrick Pantel. 2001. Discovery of inference rules for question answering. *Natural Language Engineering*, 7(4):343–360.

Dekang Lin. 1998. Dependency-based evaluation of minipar. In *Proceedings of the Workshop on Evaluation of Parsing Systems at LREC 1998*, Granada, Spain.

John B. Lowe, Collin F. Baker, and Charles J. Fillmore. 1997. A frame-semantic approach to semantic annotation. In *Proceedings of the SIGLEX Workshop on Tagging Text with Lexical Semantics: Why, What, and How?*

Catherine Macleod, Ralph Grishman, Adam Meyers, Leslie Barrett, and Ruth Reeves. 1998. NOMLEX: A Lexicon of Nominalizations. In *Proceedings of EURALEX.*

Adams Meyers, Catherine Macleod, Roman Yangarber, Ralph Grishman, Leslie Barrett, and Ruth Reeves. 1998. Using nomlex to produce nominalization patterns for information extraction. In *Proceedings of COLING.*

Adam Meyers, Ruth Reeves, Catherine Macleod, Rachel Szekeley, Veronkia Zielinska, and Brian Young. 2004. The Cross-Breeding of Dictionaries. In *Proceedings of LREC.*

George A. Miller. 1995. Wordnet: A lexical database for english. In *Communications of the ACM.*

Dan Moldovan and Rada Mihalcea. 2000. Using wordnet and lexical operators to improve internet searches. *IEEE Internet Computing*, 4(1):34–43.

Dan Moldovan and Adrian Novischi. 2002. Lexical chains for question answering. In *Proceedings of COLING.*

Dan Moldovan and Vasile Rus. 2001. Logic form transformation of wordnet and its applicability to question answering. In *Proceedings of ACL.*

Adrian Novischi and Dan Moldovan. 2006. Question answering with lexical chains propagating verb arguments. In *Proceedings of ACL.*

Martha Palmer, Hoa Trang Dang, and Christiane Fellbaum. 2007. Making fine-grained and coarse-grained sense distinctions, both manually and automatically. *Natural Language Engineering*, 13(2):137–163.

Marius Pasca and Sanda Harabagiu. 2001. The informative role of wordnet in open-domain question answering. In *Proceedings of Workshop on WordNet and Other Lexical Resources: Applications, Extensions and Customizations.*

Satoshi Sekine. 2005. Automatic paraphrase discovery based on context and keywords between ne pairs. In *Proceedings of IWP.*

Rion Snow, Daniel Jurafsky, and Andrew Y. Ng. 2006. Semantic taxonomy induction from heterogenous evidence. In *Proceedings of ACL.*

Fabian M. Suchanek, Gjergji Kasneci, and Gerhard Weikum. 2007. Yago: A core of semantic knowledge - unifying wordnet and wikipedia. In *Proceedings of WWW2007.*

Idan Szpektor and Ido Dagan. 2008. Learning entailment rules for unary templates. In *Proceedings of COLING.*

Idan Szpektor, Hristo Tanev, Ido Dagan, and Bonaventure Coppola. 2004. Scaling web based acquisition of entailment patterns. In *Proceedings of EMNLP 2004.*

Idan Szpektor, Ido Dagan, Roy Bar-Haim, and Jacob Goldberger. 2008. Contextual preferences. In *Proceedings of ACL.*

Frank Wilcoxon. 1945. Individual comparisons by ranking methods. *Biometrics Bulletin*, 1:80–83.

# Optimizing Textual Entailment Recognition Using Particle Swarm Optimization

**Yashar Mehdad**
University of Trento and FBK - Irst
Trento, Italy
mehdad@fbk.eu

**Bernardo Magnini**
FBK - Irst
Trento, Italy
magnini@fbk.eu

## Abstract

This paper introduces a new method to improve tree edit distance approach to textual entailment recognition, using particle swarm optimization. Currently, one of the main constraints of recognizing textual entailment using tree edit distance is to tune the cost of edit operations, which is a difficult and challenging task in dealing with the entailment problem and datasets. We tried to estimate the cost of edit operations in tree edit distance algorithm automatically, in order to improve the results for textual entailment. Automatically estimating the optimal values of the cost operations over all RTE development datasets, we proved a significant enhancement in accuracy obtained on the test sets.

## 1 Introduction

One of the main aspects of natural languages is to express the same meaning in many possible ways, which directly increase the language variability and emerges the complex structure in dealing with human languages. Almost all computational linguistics tasks such as Information Retrieval (IR), Question Answering (QA), Information Extraction (IE), text summarization and Machine Translation (MT) have to cope with this notion. Textual Entailment Recognition was proposed by (Dagan and Glickman, 2004), as a generic task in order to conquer the problem of lexical, syntactic and semantic variabilities in languages.

Textual Entailment can be explained as an association between a coherent text (T) and a language expression, called hypothesis (H) such that entailment function for the pair T-H returns the true value when the meaning of H can be inferred from the meaning of T and false, otherwise.

Amongst the approaches to the problem of textual entailment, some methods utilize the notion of distance between the pair of T and H as the main feature which separates the entailment classes (positive and negative). One of the successful algorithms implemented Tree Edit Distance (TED), based on the syntactic features that are represented in the structured parse tree of each string (Kouylekov and Magnini, 2005). In this method the distance is computed as the cost of the edit operations (insertion, deletion and substitution) that transform the text T into the hypothesis H. Each edit operation has an associated cost and the entailment score is calculated such that the set of operations would lead to the minimum cost.

Generally, the initial cost is assigned to each edit operation empirically, or based on the expert knowledge and experience. These methods emerge a critical problem when the domain, field or application is new and the level of expertise and empirical knowledge is very limited. In dealing with textual entailment, (Kouylekov and Magnini, 2006) tried to experiment different cost values based on various linguistics knowledge and probabilistics estimations. For instance, they defined the substitution cost as a function of similarity between two nodes, or, for insertion cost, they employed Inverse Document Frequency (IDF) of the inserted node. However, the results could not proven to be optimal.

Other approaches towards estimating the cost of operations in TED tried to learn a generic or discriminative probabilistic model (Bernard et al., 2008; Neuhaus and Bunke, 2004) from the data, without concerning the optimal value of each operation. One of the drawbacks of those approaches is that the cost values of edit operations are hidden behind the probabilistic model. Additionally, the cost can not be weighted or varied according to the tree context and node location (Bernard et al., 2008).

In order to overcome these drawbacks, we are proposing a stochastic method based on Particle



*Proceedings of the 2009 Workshop on Applied Textual Inference, ACL-IJCNLP 2009*, pages 36–43,
Suntec, Singapore, 6 August 2009. ©2009 ACL and AFNLP

Swarm Optimization (PSO), to estimate the cost of each edit operation for textual entailment problem. Implementing PSO, we try to learn the optimal cost for each operation in order to improve the prior textual entailment model. In this paper, the goal is to automatically estimate the best possible operation costs on the development set. A further advantage of such method, besides automatic learning of the operation costs, is being able to investigate the cost values to better understand how TED approaches the data in textual entailment.

The rest of the paper is organized as follows: After describing the TED approach to textual entailment in the next section, PSO optimization algorithm and our method in applying it to the problem are explained in sections 4 and 5. Then we present our experimental setup as well as the results, in detail. Finally, in the conclusion, the main advantages of our approach are reviewed and further developments are proposed accordingly.

## 2 Tree Edit Distance and Textual Entailment

One of the approaches to textual entailment is based on the Tree Edit Distance (TED) between T and H. The tree edit distance measure is a similarity metric for rooted ordered trees. This metric was initiated by (Tai, 1979) as a generalization of the string edit distance problem and was improved by (Zhang and Shasha, 1989) and (Klein, 1998).

The distance is computed as the cost of editing operations (i.e. insertion, deletion and substitution), which are required to transform the text T into the hypothesis H, while each edit operation on two text fragments A and B (denoted as $A \to B$) has an associated cost (denoted as $\gamma$ ($A \to$ B)). In textual entailment context, the edit operations are defined in the following way based on the dependency parse tree of T and H:

- Insertion ($\lambda \to A$): insert a node A from the dependency tree of H into the dependency tree of T. When a node is inserted it is attached to the dependency relation of the source label.
- Deletion ($A \to \lambda$): delete a node A from the dependency tree of T. When A is deleted all its children are attached to the parent of A. It is not required to explicitly delete the children of A, as they are going to be either deleted or substituted in a following step.
- Substitution ($A \to B$): change the label of a node A in the source tree into a label of a node B of the target tree. In the case of substitution, the relation attached to the substituted node is changed with the relation of the new node.

According to (Zhang and Shasha, 1989), the minimum cost mappings of all the descendants of each node has to be computed before the node is encountered, so the least-cost mapping can be selected right away. To accomplish this the algorithm keeps track of the keyroots of the tree, which are defined as a set that contains the root of the tree plus all nodes which have a left sibling. This problem can be easily solved using recursive methods (Selkow, 1977), or as it was suggested in (Zhang and Shasha, 1989) by dynamic programming. (Zhang and Shasha, 1989) defined the relevant subproblems of tree $T$ as the prefixes of all special subforests rooted in the keyroots. This approach computes the TED ($\delta$) by the following equations:

$$\delta(F_T,\theta) = \delta(F_T - r_{F_T},\theta) + \gamma(r_{F_T} \to \lambda) \quad (1)$$

$$\delta(\theta,F_H) = \delta(\theta,F_H - r_{F_H}) + \gamma(\lambda \to r_{F_H}) \quad (2)$$

$$\delta(F_T,F_H) = min \begin{cases} \delta(F_T - r_{F_T}, F_H) + \gamma(r_{F_T} \to \lambda) \\ \delta(F_T, F_H - r_{F_H}) + \gamma(\lambda \to r_{F_H}) \\ \delta(F_T(r_{F_T}), F_H(r_{F_H})) + \\ \delta(F_T - T(r_{F_T}), F_H - H(r_{F_H})) + \\ \gamma(r_{F_T} \to r_{F_H}) \end{cases} \quad (3)$$

where $F_T$ and $F_H$ are forests of $T$ and $H$, while $r_{F_T}$ and $r_{F_H}$ are the rightmost roots of the trees in $F_T$ and $F_H$ respectively. $\theta$ is an empty forest. Moreover, $F_T(r_{F_T})$ and $F_H(r_{F_H})$ are the forests rooted in $r_{F_T}$ and $r_{F_H}$ respectively.

Estimating $\delta$ as the bottom line of the computation is directly related to the cost of each operation. Moreover, the cost of edit operations can simply change the way that a tree is transformed to another. As Figure 1[1] shows (Demaine et al., 2007), there could exist more than one edit script for transforming each tree to another. Based on the

[1] The example adapted from (Demaine et al., 2007)

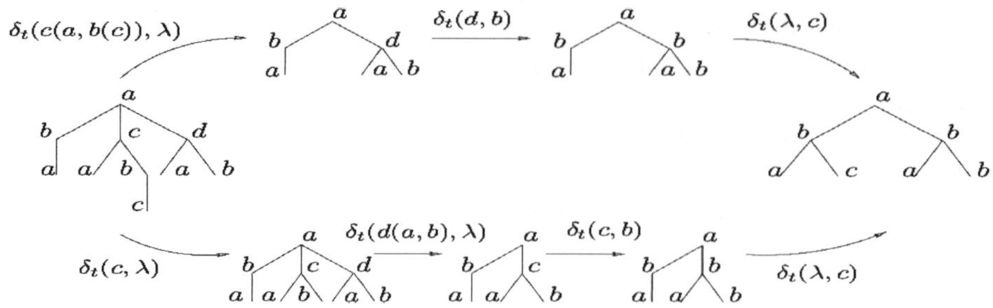


Figure 1: Two possible edit scripts to transform one tree to another.

main definition of this approach, TED is the cost of minimum cost edit script between two trees.

The entailment score for a pair is calculated on the minimal set of edit operations that transform the dependency parse tree of T into H. An entailment relation is assigned to a T-H pair where the overall cost of the transformations is below a certain threshold. The threshold, which corresponds to tree edit distace, is empirically estimated over the dataset. This method was implemented by (Kouylekov and Magnini, 2005), based on the algorithm by (Zhang and Shasha, 1989).

In this method, a cost value is assigned to each operation initially, and the distance is computed based on the initial cost values. Considering that the distance can vary in different datasets, converging to an optimal set of values for operations is almost empirically impossible. In the following sections, we propose a method for estimating the optimum set of values for operation costs in TED algorithm dealing with textual entailment problem. Our method is built on adapting PSO optimization approach as a search process to automate the procedure of the cost estimation.

## 3 Particle Swarm Optimization

PSO is a stochastic optimization technique which was introduced based on the social behaviour of bird flocking and fish schooling (Eberhart et al., 2001). It is one of the population-based search methods which takes advantage of the concept of social sharing of information. The main structure of this algorithm is not very different from other evolutionary techniques such as Genetic Algorithms (GA); however, the easy implementation and less complexity of PSO, as two main characteristics, are good motivations to apply this optimization approach in many areas.

In this algorithm each *particle* can learn from the experience of other particles in the same population (called *swarm*). In other words, each particle in the iterative search process, would adjust its flying velocity as well as position not only based on its own acquaintance, but also other particles' flying experience in the swarm. This algorithm has found efficient in solving a number of engineering problems. In the following, we briefly explain the main concepts of PSO.

To be concise, for each particle at each iteration, the position $X_i$ (Equation 4) and velocity $V_i$ (Equation 5) is updated. $X_{bi}$ is the best position of the particle during its past routes and $X_{gi}$ is the best global position over all routes travelled by the particles of the swarm. $r_1$ and $r_2$ are random variables drawn from a uniform distribution in the range [0,1], while $c_1$ and $c_2$ are two acceleration constants regulating the relative velocities with respect to the best local and global positions. The weight $\omega$ is used as a tradeoff between the global and local best positions and its value is usually selected slightly less than 1 for better global exploration (Melgani and Bazi, 2008). The optimal position is computed based on the fitness function defined in association with the related problem. Both position and velocity are updated during the iterations until convergence is reached or iterations attain the maximum number defined by the user. This search process returns the best fitness function over the particles, which is defined as the optimized solution.

$$X_i = X_i + V_i \tag{4}$$

$$V_i = \omega V_i + c_1 r_1 (X_{bi} - X_i) + c_2 r_2 (X_{gi} - X_i) \tag{5}$$

Algorithm 1 shows a simple pseudo code of how this optimization algorithm works. In the rest of the paper, we describe our method to integrate this algorithm with TED.

**Algorithm 1** PSO algorithm

**for all** *particles* **do**
  *Initialize particle*
**end for**
**while** *Convergence or maximum iteration* **do**
  **for all** *particles* **do**
    *Calculate fitness function*
    **if** *fitness function value* $> X_{bi}$ **then**
      $X_{bi} \Leftarrow$ *fitness function value*
    **end if**
  **end for**
  *choose the best particle amongst all in* $X_{gi}$
  **for all** *particles* **do**
    *calculate* $V_i$
    *update* $X_i$
  **end for**
**end while**
**return** *best particle*

## 4 Automatic Cost Estimation

One of the challenges in applying TED for recognizing textual entailment is estimating the cost of each edit operation which transforms the text T into the hypothesis H in an entailment pair. Since the cost of edit operations can directly affect the distance, which is the main criteria to measure the entailment, it is not trivial to estimate the cost of each operation. Moreover, considering that implying different costs for edit operations can affect the results in different data sets and approaches, it motivates the idea of optimizing the cost values.

### 4.1 PSO Setup

One of the most important steps in applying PSO is to define a fitness function which could lead the swarm to the optimized particles based on the application and data. The choice of this function is very crucial, since PSO evaluates the quality of each candidate particle for driving the solution space to optimization, on the basis of the fitness function. Moreover, this function should possibly improve the textual entailment recognition model. In order to attain these goals, we tried to define two main fitness functions as follows.

1. **Bhattacharyya Distance**: This measure was proposed by (Bhattacharyya, 1943) as a statistical measure to determine the similarity or distance between two discrete probability distributions. In binary classification, this method is widely used to measure the distance between two different classes. In the studies by (Fukunaga, 1990), Bhattacharyya distance was occluded to be one of the most effective measure specifically for estimating the separability of two classes. Figure 2 shows the intuition behind this measure.

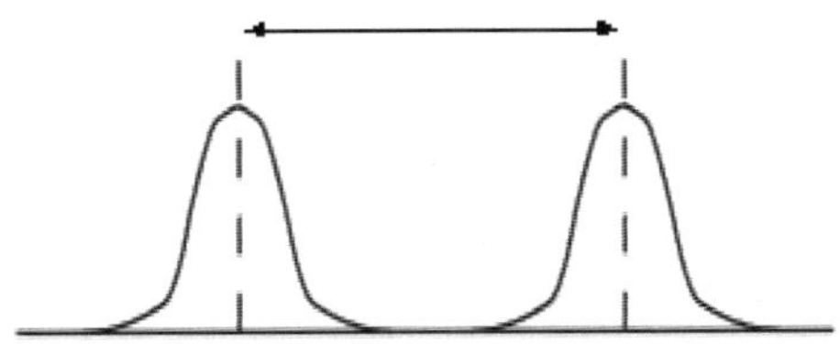

Figure 2: Bhattacharyya distance between two classes with similar variances.

   Bhattacharyya distance is calculated based on the covariance ($\sigma$) and mean ($\mu$) of each distribution based on its simplest formulation in Equation 6 (Reyes-Aldasoro and Bhalerao, 2006). Maximizing the distance between the classes would result a better separability which aims to a better classification results. Furthermore, estimating the costs using this function would indirectly improve the performance specially in classification problems. It could be stated that, maximizing the Bhattacharyya distance would increase the separability of two entailment classes which result in a better performance.

$$BD(c_1, c_2) = \frac{1}{4} ln\{\frac{1}{4}(\frac{\sigma_{c_1}^2}{\sigma_{c_2}^2} + \frac{\sigma_{c_2}^2}{\sigma_{c_1}^2} + 2)\} + \frac{1}{4}\{\frac{(\mu_{c_1} - \mu_{c_2})^2}{\sigma_{c_1}^2 + \sigma_{c_2}^2}\} \quad (6)$$

2. **Accuracy**: Accuracy or any performance measure obtained from a TED based system, can define a good fitness function in optimizing the cost values. Since maximizing the accuracy would directly increase the performance of the system or enhance the model to solve the problem, this measure is a possible choice to adapt in order to achieve our aim. In this method, trying to maximize the fitness function will compute the best model based on the optimal cost values in the particle space of PSO algorithm.

   In other words, by defining the accuracy obtained from 10 fold cross-validation over the development set, as the fitness function, we could estimate the optimized cost of the edit operations. Maximizing the accuracy gained in this way, would lead to find the set of edit operation costs which directly increases our accuracy, and consequently guides us to the main goal of optimization.

In the following section, the procedure of estimating the optimal costs are described in detail.

### 4.2 Integrating TED with PSO for Textual Entailment Problem

The procedure describing the proposed system to optimize and estimate the cost of edit operations in TED applying PSO algorithm is as follows.

a) *Initialization*

Step 1) Generate a random swarm of particles (in a simple case each particle is defined by the cost of three operations).

Step 2) For each position of the particle from the swarm, obtain the fitness function value (Bhattacharyya distance or accuracy) over the training data.

Step 3) Set the best position of each particle with its initial position ($X_{bi}$).

b) *Search*

Step 4) Detect the best global position ($X_{gi}$) in the swarm based on maximum value of the fitness function over all explored routes.

Step 5) Update the velocity of each particle ($V_i$).

Step 6) Update the position of each particle ($X_i$). In this step, by defining the boundaries, we could stop the particle to exit the allowed search space.

Step 7) For each candidate particle calculate the fitness function (Bhattacharyya distance or accuracy).

Step 8) Update the best position of each particle if the current position has a larger value.

c) *Convergence*

Step 9) Run till the maximum number of iteration (in our case set to 10) is reached or start the search process.

d) *Results*

Step 10) Return the best fitness function value and the best particle. In this step the optimum costs are returned.

Following the steps above, in contrary to determine the entailment relation applying tree edit distance, the operation costs can be automatically estimated and optimized. In this process, both fitness functions could be easily compared and the cost values leading to the better model would be selected. In the following section, the experimental procedure for obtaining the optimal costs by exploiting the PSO approach to TE is described.

## 5 Experimental Design

In our experiments we show an increase in the performance of TED based approach to textual entailment, by optimizing the cost of edit operations. In the following subsections, the framework and dataset of our experiments are elaborated.

### 5.1 Dataset Description

Our experiments were conducted on the basis of the Recognizing Textual Entailment (RTE) datasets[2], which were developed under PASCAL RTE challenge. Each RTE dataset includes its own development and test set, however, RTE-4 was released only as a test set and the data from RTE-1 to RTE-3 were used as development set. More details about the RTE datasets are illustrated in Table 5.1.

| | Number of pairs | | | |
|---|---|---|---|---|
| | Development | | Test | |
| Datasets | YES | NO | YES | NO |
| RTE-1 | 283 | 284 | 400 | 400 |
| RTE-2 | 400 | 400 | 400 | 400 |
| RTE-3 | 412 | 388 | 410 | 390 |
| RTE-4 | — | — | 500 | 500 |

Table 1: RTE-1 to RTE-4 datasets.

### 5.2 Experimental Framework

In our experiments, in order to deal with TED approach to textual entailment, we used EDITS[3] package (Edit Distance Textual Entailment Suite)

[2]http://www.pascal-network.org/Challenges/RTE1-4

[3]The EDITS system has been supported by the EU-funded project QALL-ME (FP6 IST-033860). Available at http://edits.fbk.eu/

(Magnini et al., 2009). This system is an open source software based on edit distance algorithms, and computes the T-H distance as the cost of the edit operations (i.e. insertion, deletion and substitution) that are necessary to transform T into H. By defining the edit distance algorithm and a cost scheme (assigning a cost to the edit operations), this package is able to learn a TED threshold, over a set of string pairs, to decide if the entailment exists in a pair.

In addition, we partially exploit the JSwarm-PSO[4] (Cingolani, 2005) package, with some adaptations, as an implementation of PSO algorithm. Each pair in the datasets is converted to two syntactic dependency parse trees using the Stanford statistical parser[5], developed in the Stanford university NLP group by (Klein and Manning, 2003).

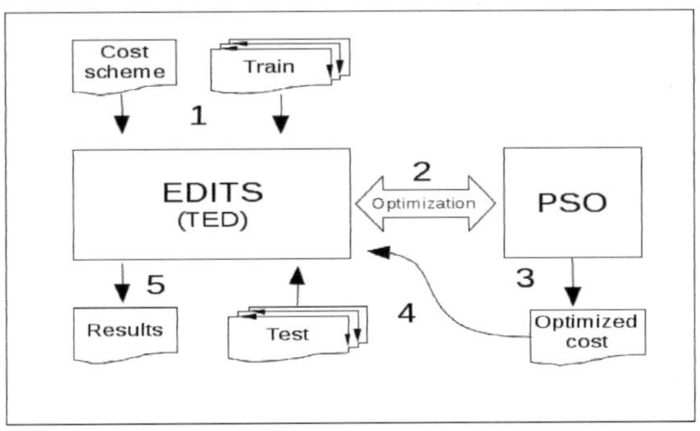


Figure 3: Five main steps of the experimental framework.

In order to take advantage of PSO optimization approach, we integrated EDITS and JSwarm-PSO to provide a flexible framework for the experiments (Figure 5.3). In this way, we applied the defined fitness functions in the integrated system. The Bhattacharyya distance between two classes (YES and NO), in each experiment, could be computed based on the TED score of each pair in the dataset. Moreover, the accuracy, by default, is computed by EDITS over the training set based on 10-fold cross-validation.

### 5.3 Experimental Scheme

We conducted six different experiments in two sets on each RTE dataset. The costs were estimated on the training set and the results obtained based on the estimated costs over the test set. In the first set of experiments, we set a simple cost scheme based on three operations. Implementing this cost scheme, we expect to optimize the cost of each edit operation without considering that the operation costs may vary based on different characteristics of a node, such as size, location or content. The results were obtained considering three different settings: 1) the random cost assignment; 2) assigning the cost based on the human expertise knowledge and intuition (called Intuitive), and 3) automatic estimated and optimized cost for each operation. In the second case, we used the same scheme which was used in EDITS by its developers (Magnini et al., 2009).

In the second set of experiments, we tried to compose an advanced cost scheme with more fine-grained operations to assign a weight to the edit operations based on the characteristics of the nodes. For example if a node is in the list of stop-words, the deletion cost is set to zero. Otherwise, the cost of deletion would be equal to the number of words in H multiplied by word's length (number of characters). Similarly, the cost of inserting a word w in H is set to 0 if w is a stop word, and to the number of words in T multiplied by words length otherwise. The cost of substituting two words is the Levenshtein distance (i.e. the edit distance calculated at the level of characters) between their lemmas, multiplied by the number of words in T, plus number of words in H. By this intuition, we tried to optimize nine specialized costs for edit operations (i.e. each particle is defined by 9 parameters to be optimized). We conducted the experiments using all three cases mentioned in the simple cost scheme.

In each experiment, we applied both fitness functions in the optimization; however, at the final phase, the costs which led to the maximum results were chosen as the estimated operation costs. In order to save breath and time, we set the number of iterations to 10, in addition, the weight $\omega$ was set to 0.95 for better global exploration (Melgani and Bazi, 2008).

## 6 Results

Our results are summarized in Table 2. We show the accuracy gained by a distance-based (word-overlap) baseline for textual entailment (Mehdad and Magnini, 2009) to be compared with the results achieved by the random, intuitive and optimized cost schemes using EDITS system. For

[4]http://jswarm-pso.sourceforge.net/

[5]http://nlp.stanford.edu/software/lex-parser.shtml

| Model | | Data set RTE-4 | RTE-3 | RTE-2 | RTE-1 |
|---|---|---|---|---|---|
| Simple | Random | 49.6 | 53.62 | 50.37 | 50.5 |
| | Intuitive | 51.3 | 59.6 | 56.5 | 49.8 |
| | Optimized | 56.5 | 61.62 | 58 | 58.12 |
| Advanced | Random | 53.60 | 52.0 | 54.62 | 53.5 |
| | Intuitive | 57.6 | 59.37 | 57.75 | 55.5 |
| | Optimized | 59.5 | 62.4 | 59.87 | 58.62 |
| Baseline | | 55.2 | 60.9 | 54.8 | 51.4 |
| RTE-4 Challenge | | 57.0 | | | |

Table 2: Comparison of accuracy on all RTE datasets based on optimized and unoptimized cost schemes.

the better comparison, we also present the results of the EDITS system in RTE-4 challenge using a combination of different distances as features for classification (Cabrio et al., 2008).

In the first experiment, we estimated the cost of each operation using the simple cost scheme. Table 2 shows that in all datasets, accuracy improved up to 9% by optimizing the cost of each edit operation. Results prove that the optimized cost scheme enhances the quality of the system performance, even more than the cost scheme used by experts (Intuitive cost scheme) (Magnini et al., 2009).

Furthermore, in the second set of experiments, using the fine-grained and weighted cost scheme for edit operations we could achieve the highest results in accuracy. The chart in Figure 4, illustares that all optimized results outperform the word-overlap baseline for textual entailment as well as the accuracy obtained in RTE-4 challenge using combination of different distances as features for classification (Cabrio et al., 2008).

By exploring the estimated optimal cost of each operation, another interesting point was discovered. The estimated cost of deletion in the first set of experiments was 0, which means that deleting a node from the dependency tree of T does not effect the quality of results. This proves that by setting different cost schemes, we could explore even some linguistics phenomena which exists in the entailment dataset. Studying the dataset from this point of view might be interesting to find some hidden information which can not be explored easily.

In addition, the optimized model can reflect more consistency and stability (from 58 to 62 in accuracy) than other models, while in unoptimized models the result varies more, on different datasets (from 50 in RTE-1 to 59 in RTE-3). Moreover, we believe that by changing some parameters such as maximum number of iterations, or by defining a better cost scheme, there could be still a room for improvement.

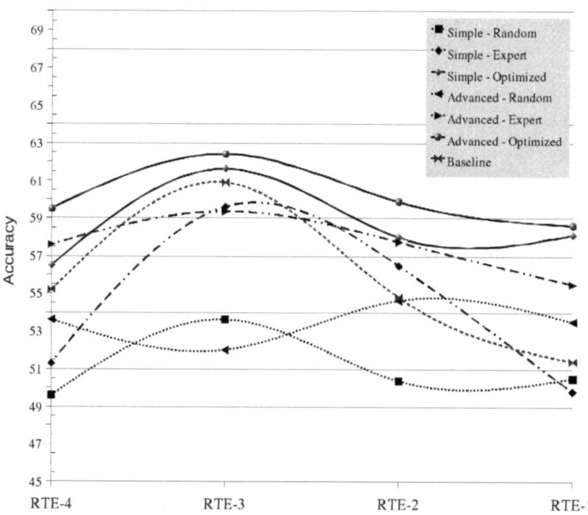


Figure 4: Accuracy obtained by different experimental setups.

## 7 Conclusion

In this paper, we proposed a novel approach for estimating the cost of edit operations for the tree edit distance approach to textual entailment. With this work we illustrated another step forward in improving the foundation of working with distance-based algorithms for textual entailment. The experimental results confirm our working hypothesis that by improving the results in applying tree edit distance for textual entailment, besides outperforming the distance-based baseline for recognizing textual entailment.

We believe that for further development, extending the cost scheme to find weighted and specialized cost operations to deal with different cases, can lead to more interesting results. Besides that, exploring and studying the estimated cost of operations, could be interesting from a linguistics point of view.

## Acknowledgments

Besides my special thanks to Farid Melgani for his helpful ideas, I acknowledge Milen Kouylekov for his academic and technical supports. This work has been partially supported by the three-year project LiveMemories (http://www.livememories.org/), funded by the Provincia Autonoma di Trento.

## References

Marc Bernard, Laurent Boyer, Amaury Habrard, and Marc Sebban. 2008. Learning probabilistic models of tree edit distance. *Pattern Recogn.*, 41(8):2611–2629.

A. Bhattacharyya. 1943. On a measure of divergence between two statistical populations defined by probability distributions. *Bull. Calcutta Math. Soc.*, 35:99109.

Elena Cabrio, Milen Kouylekovand, and Bernardo Magnini. 2008. Combining specialized entailment engines for rte-4. In *Proceedings of TAC08, 4th PASCAL Challenges Workshop on Recognising Textual Entailment.*

Pablo Cingolani. 2005. Jswarm-pso: Particle swarm optimization package. Available at http://jswarm-pso.sourceforge.net/.

Ido Dagan and Oren Glickman. 2004. Probabilistic textual entailment: Generic applied modeling of language variability. In *Proceedings of the PASCAL Workshop of Learning Methods for Text Understanding and Mining.*

E. Demaine, S. Mozes, B. Rossman, and O. Weimann. 2007. An optimal decomposition algorithm for tree edit distance. In *Proceedings of the 34th International Colloquium on Automata, Languages and Programming (ICALP)*, pages 146–157.

Russell C. Eberhart, Yuhui Shi, and James Kennedy. 2001. *Swarm Intelligence.* The Morgan Kaufmann Series in Artificial Intelligence. Morgan Kaufmann.

Keinosuke Fukunaga. 1990. *Introduction to statistical pattern recognition (2nd ed.).* Academic Press Professional, Inc., San Diego, CA, USA.

Dan Klein and Christopher D. Manning. 2003. Fast exact inference with a factored model for natural language parsing. In *Advances in Neural Information Processing Systems 15*, pages 3–10, Cambridge, MA. MIT Press.

Philip N. Klein. 1998. Computing the edit-distance between unrooted ordered trees. In *ESA '98: Proceedings of the 6th Annual European Symposium on Algorithms*, pages 91–102, London, UK. Springer-Verlag.

Milen Kouylekov and Bernardo Magnini. 2005. Recognizing textual entailment with tree edit distance algorithms. In *PASCAL Challenges on RTE*, pages 17–20.

Milen Kouylekov and Bernardo Magnini. 2006. Tree edit distance for recognizing textual entailment: Estimating the cost of insertion. In *PASCAL RTE-2 Challenge.*

Bernardo Magnini, Milen Kouylekov, and Elena Cabrio. 2009. Edits - edit distance textual entailment suite user manual. Available at http://edits.fbk.eu/.

Yashar Mehdad and Bernardo Magnini. 2009. A word overlap baseline for the recognizing textual entailment task. Available at http://edits.fbk.eu/.

Farid Melgani and Yakoub Bazi. 2008. Classification of electrocardiogram signals with support vector machines and particle swarm optimization. *IEEE Transactions on Information Technology in Biomedicine*, 12(5):667–677.

Michel Neuhaus and Horst Bunke. 2004. A probabilistic approach to learning costs for graph edit distance. In *ICPR '04*, pages 389–393, Washington, DC, USA. IEEE Computer Society.

C. C. Reyes-Aldasoro and A. Bhalerao. 2006. The bhattacharyya space for feature selection and its application to texture segmentation. *Pattern Recogn.*, 39(5):812–826.

Stanley M. Selkow. 1977. The tree-to-tree editing problem. *Inf. Process. Lett.*, 6(6):184–186.

Kuo-Chung Tai. 1979. The tree-to-tree correction problem. *J. ACM*, 26(3):422–433.

K. Zhang and D. Shasha. 1989. Simple fast algorithms for the editing distance between trees and related problems. *SIAM J. Comput.*, 18(6):1245–1262.

# Ranking Paraphrases in Context

**Stefan Thater**
Universität des Saarlandes
stth@coli.uni-sb.de

**Georgiana Dinu**
Universität des Saarlandes
dinu@coli.uni-sb.de

**Manfred Pinkal**
Universität des Saarlandes
pinkal@coli.uni-sb.de

## Abstract

We present a vector space model that supports the computation of appropriate vector representations for words in context, and apply it to a paraphrase ranking task. An evaluation on the SemEval 2007 lexical substitution task data shows promising results: the model significantly outperforms a current state of the art model, and our treatment of context is effective.

## 1 Introduction

Knowledge about paraphrases is of central importance to textual inference modeling. Systems which support automatic extraction of large repositories of paraphrase or inference rules like Lin and Pantel (2001) or Szpektor et al. (2004) thus form first-class candidate resources to be leveraged for NLP tasks like question answering, information extraction, or summarization, and the meta-task of recognizing textual entailment.

Existing knowledge bases still suffer a number of limitations, making their use in applications challenging. One of the most serious problems is insensitivity to context. Natural-language inference is highly context-sensitive, the applicability of inference rules depending on word sense and even finer grained contextual distinctions in usage (Szpektor et al., 2007). Application of a rule like "*X shed Y* ⇔ *X throw Y*" is appropriate in a sentence like "a mouse study sheds light on the mixed results," but not in sentences like "the economy seems to be shedding fewer jobs" or "cats do not shed the virus to other cats." Systems like the above-mentioned ones base the extraction of inference rules on distributional similarity of words rather than word senses, and apply unconditionally whenever one side of the rule matches on the word level, which may lead to considerable precision problems (Geffet and Dagan, 2005) .

Some approaches address the problem of context sensitivity by deriving inference rules whose argument slots bear selectional preference information (Pantel et al., 2007; Basili et al., 2007). A different line of accounting for contextual variation has been taken by Mitchell and Lapata (2008), who propose a compositional approach, "contextualizing" the vector-space meaning representation of predicates by combining the distributional properties of the predicate with those of its arguments. A related approach has been proposed by Erk and Padó (2008), who integrate selectional preferences into the compositional picture. In this paper, we propose a context-sensitive vector-space approach which draws some important ideas from Erk and Pado's paper ("E&P" in the following), but implements them in a different, more effective way: An evaluation on the SemEval 2007 lexical substitution task data shows that our model significantly outperforms E&P in terms of average precision.

**Plan of the paper.** Section 2 presents our model and briefly relates it to previous work. Section 3 describes the evaluation of our model on the lexical substitution task data. Section 4 concludes.

## 2 A model for meaning in context

We propose a dependency-based model whose dimensions reflect dependency relations, and distinguish two kinds or layers of lexical meaning: *argument meaning* and *predicate meaning*. The argument meaning of a word $w$ is a vector representing frequencies of all pairs $(w', r')$ of predicate expressions $w'$ and dependency relations $r'$ such that $w'$ stands in relation $r'$ to $w$. Intuitively, argument meaning is similar to E&P's "inverse selectional preferences." Argument meanings are used for two purposes in our model: (i) to construct predicate meanings, and (ii) to contextually constrain them.

For technical convenience, we will use a definitional variant of argument meaning, by indexing it with an "incoming" relation, which allows predicate and argument meaning to be treated technically as vectors of the same type. Assuming a set



*Proceedings of the 2009 Workshop on Applied Textual Inference, ACL-IJCNLP 2009*, pages 44–47,
Suntec, Singapore, 6 August 2009. 

$R$ of role labels and a set $W$ of words, we represent both predicate and argument meaning as vectors in a vector space $V$ with a basis $\{e_i\}_{i \in R \times R \times W}$, i.e., a vector space whose dimensions correspond to triples of two role labels and a word. The argument meaning $v_r(w)$ of a word $w$ is defined as follows:

$$v_r(w) = \sum_{w' \in W, r' \in R} f(w', r', w) \cdot e_{(r, r', w')}, \quad (1)$$

where $r$ is the "incoming" relation, and $f(w', r', w)$ denotes the frequency of $w$ occurring in relation $r'$ to $w'$ in a collection of dependency trees. To obtain predicate meaning $v_P(w)$, we count the occurrences of argument words $w'$ standing in relation $r$ to $w$, and compute the predicate meaning as the sum of the argument meanings $v_r(w')$, weighted by these co-occurrence frequencies:

$$v_P(w) = \sum_{r \in R, w' \in W} f(w, r, w') \cdot v_r(w') \quad (2)$$

That is, the meaning of a predicate is modelled by a vector representing "second order" co-coccurrence frequencies with other predicates.

In general, words have both a "downward looking" predicate meaning and an "upward looking" argument meaning. In our study, only one of them will be relevant, since we will restrict ourselves to local predicate-argument structures with verbal heads and nominal arguments.

**Computing meaning in context.** Vectors representing predicate meaning are derived by collecting co-occurrence frequencies for all uses of the predicate, possibly resulting in vector representations in which different meanings of the predicate are combined. Given an instance of a predicate $w$ that has arguments $w_1, \ldots, w_k$, we can now contextually constrain the predicate meaning of $w$ by the argument meanings of its arguments. Here, we propose to simple "restrict" the predicate meaning to those dimensions that have a non-zero value in at least one of its argument meanings. More formally, we write $v_{|v'}$ to denote a vector that is identical to $v$ for all components that have a non-zero value in $v'$, zero otherwise. We compute *predicate meaning in context* as follows:

$$v_P(w)_{|\sum_{1 \leq i \leq k} v_{r_i}(w_i)}, \quad (3)$$

where $r_i$ is the argument position filled by $w_i$.

**Parameters.** To reduce the effect of noise and provide a more fine-grained control over the effect of context, we can choose different thresholds for function $f$ in the computation of predicate and argument meaning. In Section 3, we obtain best results if we consider only dependency relations that occur at least 6 times in the British National Corpus (BNC) for the computation of predicate meaning, and relations occurring at least 15 times for the computation of argument meanings when predicate meaning is contextually constrained.

**Related work.** Our model is similar to the structured vector space model proposed by Erk and Padó (2008) in that the representation of predicate meaning is based on dependency relations, and that "inverse selectional preferences" play an important role. However, inverse selectional preferences are used in E&P's model mainly to compute meaning in context, while they are directly "built into" the vectors representing predicate meaning in our model.

| *target* | *subject* | *object* | *paraphrases* |
|---|---|---|---|
| shed | study | light | throw 3, reveal 2, shine 1 |
| shed | cat | virus | spread 2, pass 2, emit 1, transmit 2 |
| shed | you | blood | lose 3, spill 1, give 1 |

Table 1: Lexical substitution task data set

## 3 Evaluation

We evaluate our model on a paraphrase ranking task on a subset of the SemEval 2007 lexical substitution task (McCarthy and Navigli, 2007) data, and compare it to a random baseline and E&P's state of the art model.

**Dataset.** The lexical substitution task dataset contains 10 instances for 44 target verbs in different sentential contexts. Systems that participated in the task had to generate paraphrases for each of these instances, which are evaluated against a gold standard containing up to 9 possible paraphrases for individual instances. Following Erk and Padó (2008), we use the data in a different fashion: we pool paraphrases for all instances of a verb in all contexts, and use the models to rank these paraphrase candidates in specific contexts.

Table 1 shows three instances of the target verb *shed* together with its paraphrases in the gold standard as an expample. The paraphrases are attached with weights, which correspond to the number of times they have been given by different annotators.

To allow for a comparision with E&P's model, we follow Erk and Padó (2008) and extract only sentences from the dataset containing target verbs with overtly realized subject and object, and remove instances from the dataset for which the target verb or one of its arguments is not in the BNC. We obtain a set of 162 instances for 34 different verbs. We also remove paraphrases that are not in the BNC. On average, target verbs have 20.5 paraphrase candidates, 3.9 of which are correct in specific contexts.

**Experimental setup.** We parse the BNC using MiniPar (Lin, 1993) and extract co-occurrence frequencies, considering only dependency relations for the most frequent 2000 verbs. We don't use raw frequency counts directly but reweight the vectors by pointwise mutual information.

To rank paraphrases in context, we compute contextually constrained vectors for the verb in the input sentence and all its paraphrase candidates by taking the corresponding predicate vectors and restricting them to the argument meanings of the argument head nouns in the input sentence. The restricted vectors for the paraphrase candidates are then ranked by comparing them to the restricted vector of the input verb using cosine similarity.

In order to compare our model with state of the art, we reimplement E&P's structured vector space model. We filter stop words, and compute lexical vectors in a "syntactic" space using the most frequent 2000 words from the BNC as basis. We also consider a variant in which the basis corresponds to words indexed by their grammatical roles. We choose parameters that Erk and Padó (2009) report to perform best, and use the method described in Erk and Padó (2009) to compute vectors in context.

**Evaluation metrics.** As scoring methods, we use both "precision out of ten" ($P_{oot}$), which was originally used in the lexical substitution task and also used by E&P, and *generalized average precision* (Kishida, 2005), a variant of *average precision* which is frequently used in information extraction tasks and has also been used in the PASCAL RTE challenges (Dagan et al., 2006).

$P_{oot}$ can be defined as follows:

$$P_{oot} = \frac{\Sigma_{s \in M \cap G} f(s)}{\Sigma_{s \in G} f(s)},$$

where $M$ is the list of 10 paraphrase candidates top-ranked by the model, $G$ is the corresponding annotated gold data, and $f(s)$ is the weight of the individual paraphrases. Here, $P_{oot}$ is computed for each target instance separately; below, we report the average over all instances.

| *Model* | $P_{oot}$ | *GAP* |
|---|---|---|
| Random baseline | 54.25 | 26.03 |
| E&P (target only) | 64.61 (63.31) | 29.95 (32.02) |
| E&P (add, object only) | **66.20** (62.90) | 29.93 (31.54) |
| E&P (min, both) | 64.86 (59.62) | **32.22** (31.28) |
| TDP | 63.32 | **36.54** |
| TDP (target only) | 62.60 | 33.04 |

Table 2: Results

Generalized average precision (*GAP*) is a more precise measure than $P_{oot}$: Applied to a ranking task with about 20 candidates, $P_{oot}$ just gives the percentage of good candidates found in the upper half of the proposed ranking. Average precision is sensitive to the relative position of correct and incorrect candidates in the ranking, *GAP* moreover rewards the correct order of positive cases w.r.t. their gold standard weight.

We define average precision first:

$$AP = \frac{\Sigma_{i=1}^{n} x_i \, p_i}{R} \qquad p_i = \frac{\Sigma_{k=1}^{i} x_k}{i}$$

where $x_i$ is a binary variable indicating whether the $i$th item as ranked by the model is in the gold standard or not, $R$ is the size of the gold standard, and $n$ the number of paraphrase candidates to be ranked. If we take $x_i$ to be the gold standard weight of the $i$th item or zero if it is not in the gold standard, we can define *generalized average precision* as follows:

$$GAP = \frac{\Sigma_{i=1}^{n} I(x_i) \, p_i}{R'} \qquad R' = \Sigma_{i=1}^{R} I(y_i)\bar{y}_i$$

where $I(x_i) = 1$ if $x_i$ is larger than zero, zero otherwise, and $\bar{y}_i$ is the average weight of the ideal ranked list $y_1, \ldots, y_i$ of paraphrases in the gold standard.

**Results and discussion.** Table 2 shows the results of our experiments for two variants of our model ("TDP"), and compares them to a random baseline and three instantiations (in two variants) of E&P's model. The "target only" models don't use context information, i.e., paraphrases are ranked by cosine similarity of predicate meaning only. The other models take context into account. The "min" E&P model takes the component-wise minimum to combine a lexical vector with context vectors and considers both subject and object as context; it is the best performing model in Erk and Padó (2009). The "add" model uses vector addition and considers only objects as context; it is the best-performing

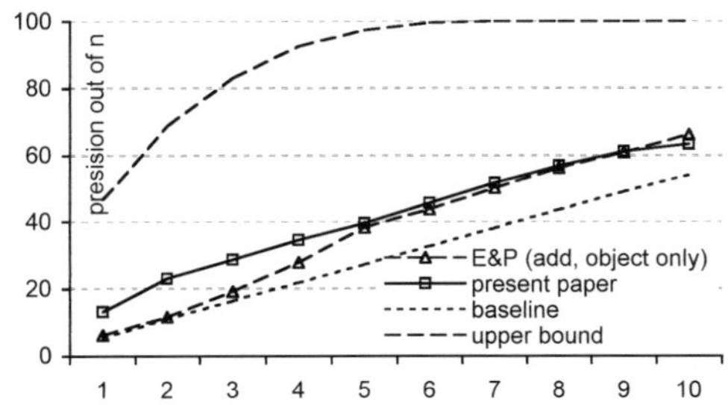


Figure 1: "Precision out of $n$" for $1 \leq n \leq 10$.

model (in terms of $P_{oot}$) for our dataset. The numbers in brackets refer to variants of the E&P models in which the basis corresponds to words indexed by their syntactic roles. Note that the results for the E&P models are better than the results published in Erk and Padó (2009), which might be due to slightly different datasets or lists of stop-words.

As can be seen, our model performs $> 10\%$ better than the random baseline. It performs $> 4\%$ better than the "min" E&P model and $> 6\%$ better then the "add" model in terms of *GAP* if we use a vectors space with words as basis. For the variants of the E&P models in which the basis corresponds to words indexed by their syntactic role, we obtain different results, but our model is still $> 4\%$ better than these variants. We can also see that our treatment of context is effective, leading to a $> 3\%$ increase of *GAP*. A stratified shuffling-based randomization test (Yeh, 2000) shows that the differences are statistically significant ($p < 0.05$).

In terms of $P_{oot}$, the "add" E&P model performs better than our model, which might look surprising, given its low *GAP* score. Fig. 1 gives a more fine-grained comparison between the two models. It displays the "precision out of $n$" of the two models for varying $n$. As can be seen, our model performs better for all $n < 10$, and much better than the baseline and E&P for $n \leq 4$.

## 4 Conclusion

In this paper, we have proposed a dependency-based context-sensitive vector-space approach that supports the computation of adequate vector-based representations of predicate meaning in context. An evaluation on a paraphrase ranking task using a subset of the SemEval 2007 lexical substitution task data shows promising results: our model performs significantly better than a current state of the art system (Erk and Padó, 2008), and our treatment of context is effective.

Since the dataset we used for the evaluation is relatively small, there is a potential danger for overfitting, and it remains to be seen whether the results carry over to larger datasets. First experiments indicate that this is actually the case.

We expect that our approach can be generalized to arrive at a general compositional model, which would allow to compute contextually appropriate meaning representations for complex relational expressions rather than single lexical predicates.

**Acknowledgements.** We thank Katrin Erk and Sebastian Padó for help and critical comments.

## References

R. Basili, D. De Cao, P. Marocco, and M. Pennacchiotti. 2007. Learning selectional preferences for entailment or paraphrasing rules. In *Proc. of RANLP 2007*.

I. Dagan, O. Glickman, and B. Magnini. 2006. The PASCAL Recognising Textual Entailment Challenge. In *Machine Learning Challenges*, volume 3944. Springer.

K. Erk and S. Padó. 2008. A structured vector space model for word meaning in context. In *Proc. of EMNLP*.

K. Erk and S. Padó. 2009. Paraphrase assessment in structured vector space: Exploring parameters and datasets. In *Proc. of the Workshop on Geometrical Models of Natural Language Semantics*, Athens.

M. Geffet and I. Dagan. 2005. The distributional inclusion hypotheses and lexical entailment. In *Proc. of the ACL*.

K. Kishida. 2005. Property of average precision and its generalization: An examination of evaluation indicator for information retrieval experiments. *NII Technical Report*.

D. Lin and P. Pantel. 2001. DIRT – Discovery of Inference Rules from Text. In *Proc. of the ACM Conference on Knowledge Discovery and Data Mining*, San Francisco.

D. Lin. 1993. Principle-based parsing without overgeneration. In *Proc. of ACL*, Columbus.

D. McCarthy and R. Navigli. 2007. SemEval-2007 Task 10: English Lexical Substitution Task. In *Proc. of SemEval*, Prague.

J. Mitchell and M. Lapata. 2008. Vector-based models of semantic composition. In *Proc. of ACL-08: HLT*, Columbus.

P. Pantel, R. Bhagat, B. Coppola, T. Chklovski, and E. Hovy. 2007. ISP: Learning inferential selectional preferences. In *Human Language Technologies 2007*, Rochester.

I. Szpektor, H. Tanev, I. Dagan, and B. Coppola. 2004. Scaling web-based acquisition of entailment relations. In *Proc. of EMNLP*, Barcellona.

I. Szpektor, E. Shnarch, and I. Dagan. 2007. Instance-based evaluation of entailment rule acquisition. In *Proc. of ACL*.

A. Yeh. 2000. More accurate tests for the statistical significance of result differences. In *Proc. of COLING*.

# Building an Annotated Textual Inference Corpus for Motion and Space

**Kirk Roberts**
Human Language Technology Research Institute
University of Texas at Dallas
Richardson TX 75080
kirk@hlt.utdallas.edu

## Abstract

This paper presents an approach for building a corpus for the domain of motion and spatial inference using a specific class of verbs. The approach creates a distribution of inference features that maximize the discriminatory power of a system trained on the corpus. The paper addresses the issue of using an existing textual inference system for generating the examples. This enables the corpus annotation method to assert whether more data is necessary.

## 1 Introduction

Open-domain textual inference provides a vast array of challenges to a textual entailment system. In order to ensure a wide distribution of these challenges in building the PASCAL 2005 corpus (Dagan et al., 2005), seven different application settings were used for inspiration: Information Retrieval, Comparable Documents, Reading Comprehension, Question Answering, Information Extraction, Machine Translation, and Paraphrase Acquisition. While PASCAL 2005 and its subsequent challenges have released numerous corpora for open-domain textual inference, many types of textual inference are sparsely represented. This speaks not to a weakness in the mentioned corpora, but rather the depth and complexity of challenges that textual inference presents.

Furthermore, the open-domain inference task often forces systems to face more than one of these challenges on a single inference pair (such as requiring both an understanding of paraphrases and part-whole relationships). In many cases, it is desirable to isolate out most of these "subtasks" within textual inference and concentrate on a single aspect. Partly for this reason, the Boeing-Princeton-ISI (BPI) Textual Entailment Test Suite[1] was developed. Its focus is real-world knowledge and not syntactic constructions, so it provides 250 syntactically simple but semantically rich inference pairs.

This paper explores the creation of such a specific textual inference corpus based on verb classes, specifically focusing on the class of *motion verbs* and their nominalizations. The goal is to develop a publicly available corpus for spatial inference involving *motion*. Section 2 analyzes the properties of such a corpus. Section 3 outlines the effort to build a motion corpus. Finally, Section 4 discusses considerations for the size of the corpus.

## 2 Properties of an Inference Corpus

### 2.1 General Properties

Annotated corpora are designed for training and evaluation for specific classification tasks, and thus an optimal corpus is one that maximizes a system's ability to form a discriminative feature space. However, knowing ahead of time what the feature space will look like may be difficult. But, at the same time the corpus should be also reflective of the real world.

One method for developing a useful corpus under these conditions, especially for a specific domain, is to use an existed textual entailment system that can aid in the example generation process. By using such a system to suggest examples, one is able to both reduce the time (and cost) of annotation as well as producing a corpus with a desirable distribution of features.

[1]Available at http://www.cs.utexas.edu/~pclark/bpi-test-suite/



*Proceedings of the 2009 Workshop on Applied Textual Inference, ACL-IJCNLP 2009*, pages 48–51,
Suntec, Singapore, 6 August 2009. 

| |
|---|
| **Text**: John flew to New York from LA.<br>**Hypothesis**: John left LA for New York. |
| **Text**: John will fly over the Atlantic during his trip to London from New York on Tuesday.<br>**Hypothesis**: On Tuesday, John flew over water when going from North America to Europe. |

Table 1: Examples of textual inference for motion.

### 2.2 Properties of a Motion Corpus

Textual inference about motion requires an external representation apart from the text. While many inference pairs can be solved with strategies such as lexical alignment or paraphrasing, many texts assume the reader has knowledge of the properties of motion. Table 1 shows two such inference pairs. The first can be solved through a paraphrase strategy, while the second requires explicit knowledge of the properties of motion that are difficult to acquire through a paraphrasing method. Unfortunately, most open-domain inference corpora are sparsely populated with such types of inference pairs, so a new corpus is required.

For the purpose of the corpus, the concept of motion is strictly limited to the set of words in the (Levin, 1993) verb-class MOTION. This greatly benefits the annotation process: passages or sentences without a verb or nominalization that fits into the MOTION class can immediately be discarded. Levin's verb classes are easily accessible via VERBNET (Kipper et al., 1998), which provides additional syntactic and semantic information as well as mappings into WORDNET (Fellbaum, 1998).

(Muller, 1998) proposes a qualitative theory of motion based on spatio-temporal primitives, while (Pustejovsky and Moszkowicz, 2008) shows an annotation structure for motion. Furthermore, representing motion requires the complete representation of spatial information, as motion is simply a continuous function that transforms space. (Hobbs and Narayanan, 2002) discuss many of the properties for spatial representation, including dimensionality, frame of reference, regions, relative location, orientation, shape, and motion. It is therefore desirable for a motion corpus to require inference over many different aspects of space as well as motion. Table 2 shows the properties of motion incorporated in the inference system.

In practice, these properties are far from uniformly distributed. Properties such as *dest*($M_x$) are far more common than *shape*($M_x$). Clearly,

| Property | Description |
|---|---|
| *motion*($M_x$) | Instance of motion in text |
| *theme*($M_x$) | Object under motion |
| *area*($M_x$) | Area of motion |
| *src*($M_x$) | Source location |
| *dest*($M_x$) | Destination location |
| *path*($M_x$) | Path of motion |
| *current*($M_x$) | Current position |
| *orientation*($M_x$) | Direction/Orientation |
| *shape*($M_x$) | Shape of object |
| *t_start*($M_x$) | Start of motion |
| *t_end*($M_x$) | End of motion |

Table 2: Extracted properties of motion.

having a system that performs well on destinations is more important than one that can draw inferences from motion's effects on an object's shape ("*the car hit the barricade and was crushed*"), but it is still desirable to have a corpus that provides systems with examples of such properties.

The corpus annotation process shall disregard many discourse-related phenomena, including coreference. Further, the text and hypothesis for each inference pair will be limited to one sentence. In this way, knowledge of motion is emphasized over other linguistic tasks.

## 3 Building a Corpus Focusing on Knowledge about Motion

To build the motion inference corpus, we chose to start with an existing, large document corpus, AQUAINT-2.[2] This corpus is composed of 2.4GB of raw files and contains over 900,000 documents. Having a large corpus is important for finding sparse verbs like *escort* and *swing* and sparse properties like *area*($M_x$) and *orientation*($M_x$).

### 3.1 Text Annotation

In order to get a more diverse distribution of motion verbs and properties (hereafter, just referred to as properties) than the given distribution from the corpus, the following procedure is considered:

Let $V_s$ be the (static) distribution of motion properties from the document corpus. Let $V_d$ be the (dynamic) distribution of motion properties from an (initially empty) set of annotated examples. Next, define a "feedback" distribution $V_f$, such that for each property $y$:

$$P_f(y) = \frac{max(0, 2P_s(y) - P_d(y))}{Z} \quad (1)$$

Where $P_s(y)$, $P_d(y)$, and $P_f(y)$ are the probabilities of property $y$ in distributions $V_s$, $V_d$, and

[2]Available through the Linguistic Data Consortium, id LDC2008T25

$V_f$, respectively, and $Z$ is a normalization factor (needed when the numerator is zero).

Let the parameter $\alpha$ determine the likelihood of sampling from this distribution $V_f$ or from the uniform distribution $U$. The function *NextExampleType($V_f$, $\alpha$)* then specifies which motion property should be in the next example. An unannotated example is then drawn from an index, annotated by the user, and placed in the set of annotated examples. $V_d$ is then updated to reflect the new distribution of verbs and properties in the annotated example set.

There are several items to note. First, the example might contain multiple properties not chosen by the *NextExampleType* method. When a motion event with a *path*($M_x$) is chosen, it is not uncommon for a *dest*($M_x$) property to be a part of the same event. This is why the $V_d$ and $V_f$ distributions are necessary: they are a feedback mechanism to try to keep the actual distribution, $V_d$, as close to the desired distribution as possible.

Second, the value for $\alpha$ is the sole pre-specified parameter. It dictates the likelihood of choosing an example despite its *a priori* probability. Setting $\alpha$ to 1.0 will result in only sampling based on the $V_f$ distribution, and setting it to 0.0 will generate a uniform sampling. In practice, this is set to 0.8 to allow many of the sparse features through.

Third, $V_d$ and $V_f$ account even for properties generated from the uniform distribution. In practice this means that low-probability events will be generated from $U$ and not $V_f$, especially later in the sampling process. Due to the non-independence of the properties as discussed above, this discrepancy is difficult to account for and is considered acceptable: $U$ will still dictate a much higher distribution of low-probability properties than would otherwise be the case.

### 3.2 Hypothesis Annotation

While the hypothesis itself must be written by the annotator, one can apply some of the same principles to ensure a coverage of motion concepts. Since not every motion term in the text need be tested by the hypothesis, it is beneficial to keep track of which properties are tested within each. For this reason, the annotator is responsible for indicating which motion properties are used in the hypothesis. This way, the annotator can be alerted to any properties under-represented in the set of hypotheses relative to the set of annotated texts.

| Feature | # | Seq | Ex Gen |
|---|---|---|---|
| *dest*($M_x$) | 749 | 48 | 60 |
| *go* | 382 | 90 | 129 |
| *leave* | 105 | 376 | 454 |
| ... | ... | ... | ... |
| *orientation*($M_x$) | 94 | 420 | 282 |
| *flee* | 4 | 9,991 | 5,508 |
| *steer* | 2 | 20,000 | 7,065 |
| *parachute* | 1 | 40,000 | 8,227 |

Table 3: Motion features with instance counts from 2000 sample sentences. The *Seq* (Sequential) and *Ex Gen* (see Section 3.1) columns are the expected number of annotated sentences for 20 instances of the feature to be found using that method, assuming i.i.d.

### 3.3 Evaluation

The purpose of the algorithm from Section 3.1 is not only to build a more balanced corpus, but to do so more quickly. By looking through examples that are more likely to maintain a balanced corpus, annotators are saved from looking through hundreds (or thousands!) of examples that contain overly redundant properties.

To illustrate this point, consider a random sample of 2000 sentences. Table 3 shows the extracted counts for some of the least and most common verbs and properties alongside projections of how many motion sentences would need to be annotated with and without the algorithm to attain a rather modest 20 examples of each. The results prove that, for many features, the example generation approach allows many more instances of that feature to be placed in the corpus.

### 3.4 Comparison with Active Learning

The process presented in Section 3.1 bears a close resemblence with active learning, so the differences between the two merit some discussion. Active learning seeks to improve a specific classifier by selecting training data based on some confidence/score metric for the purpose of improving an overall metric (usually the score across all annotated data). Often, examples on which the classifier is the least confident are presented to an annotator for manual classification. Then the system is re-trained to include the new data, and the process repeats.

The annotation process presented above, however, is not “active” in this same sense. Instead it seeks a certain distribution of properties regardless of a classifier’s ability to accurately perform inferences. The primary advantage, then, is a corpus that is not designed for a specific classification

| Corpus | # Dev | # Test |
|---|---|---|
| RTE-1 | 567 | 800 |
| RTE-2 | 800 | 800 |
| RTE-3 | 800 | 800 |
| BPI | 250 | |

Table 4: Number of annotated inferences for each inference corpus.

technique or set of features. A secondary advantage is that it avoids the risk of choosing poor examples but rather seeks a breadth of data.

## 4 Corpus Size Considerations

An important consideration–and an active area of research–is the ideal size of an annotated corpus. As one can see from Table 4, the RTE tasks make 800 examples available for an open-domain textual inference corpus.

But when the scope of the corpus is more limited, perhaps 800 examples is too few or too many. If the intent is to provide a set on which systems can be blindly evaluated for motion inference, then a much smaller number is required than a corpus intended for training machine-learned models. In this case, we seek to do the latter.

It should be mentioned that if the corpus generation process follows the algorithm presented in Section 3.1, then any reasonable number of inference pairs should follow the same distribution as a much larger set. For this reason, it is possible to adopt the active learning approach and build the corpus incrementally by iteratively annotating until satisfactory results are reached or gains are minimal.

## 5 Discussion

In addition to building a motion-specific corpus, this paper argues for the creation of domain-specific corpora for textual inference. Beyond simply measuring a system's ability to reason for specific tasks, they enable the aquisition of world knowledge through training data. They can then be used by statistical learning techniques applied to natural language processing. This is different than generating axioms and using them in abductive reasoning, which is another approach to approximate world knowledge.

Levin's verb classes (of which there are less than fifty) are a useful way to organize corpora. Levin's classes are structured under the assumption that syntactic and semantic frames are directly linked within each class. Since all verbs within the class have similar semantic arguments, knowledge aquisition becomes manageable. A system that has a wide coverage of knowledge trained on such corpora could claim a wide coverage of knowledge of all verb-based events within text.

## 6 Conclusion

This paper has presented an argument for the creation of domain-specific textual inference corpora and, in general terms, what that corpus should look like. In particular, it has described the ongoing process of building an inference corpus for spatial inference about motion. It has shown how an existing system can be used to aid in the example generation and annotation process with analysis as to the effects of the algorithm on presenting more balanced data. Finally, the paper discussed some considerations for the size of such a corpus.

Upon completion, the corpus will be made publically available.

## References

Ido Dagan, Oren Glickman, and Bernardo Magnini. 2005. The pascal recognizing textual entailment challenge. In *Proceedings of the First PASCAL Challenges Workshop on Recognising Textual Entailment*, pages 1–8.

Christiane Fellbaum, editor. 1998. *WordNet: An Electronic Lexical Database*. MIT Press.

Jerry R. Hobbs and Srini Narayanan. 2002. Spatial representation and reasoning. In *Intelligent Systems: Concepts and Applications*, pages 67–76. MacMillan.

Karin Kipper, Hoa Trang Dang, and Martha Palmer. 1998. Class-based construction of a verb lexicon. In *In Proceedings of AAAI/IAAI*.

Beth Levin. 1993. *English Verb Classes and Alternations: A Preliminary Investigation*. The University of Chicago Press.

Philippe Muller. 1998. A Qualitative Theory of Motion Based on Spatio-Temporal Primitives. In *KR '98: Principles of Knowledge Representation and Reasoning*, pages 131–141.

James Pustejovsky and Jessica L. Moszkowicz. 2008. Integrating Motion Predicate Classes with Spatial and Temporal Annotations. In *Proceedings of COLING 2008*, pages 95–98.

# Using Hypernymy Acquisition to Tackle (Part of) Textual Entailment

**Elena Akhmatova**
Centre for Language Technology
Macquarie University
Sydney, Australia
elena@ics.mq.edu.au

**Mark Dras**
Centre for Language Technology
Macquarie University
Sydney, Australia
madras@ics.mq.edu.au

## Abstract

Within the task of Recognizing Textual Entailment, various existing work has proposed the idea that tackling specific subtypes of entailment could be more productive than taking a generic approach to entailment. In this paper we look at one such subtype, where the entailment involves hypernymy relations, often found in Question Answering tasks. We investigate current work on hypernymy acquisition, and show that adapting one such approach leads to a marked improvement in entailment classification accuracy.

## 1 Introduction

The goal of the Recognizing Textual Entailment (RTE) task (Dagan et al., 2006) is, given a pair of sentences, to determine whether a Hypothesis sentence can be inferred from a Text sentence. The majority of work in RTE is focused on finding a generic solution to the task. That is, creating a system that uses the same algorithm to return a *yes* or *no* answer for all textual entailment pairs. A generic approach never works well for every single entailment pair: there are entailment pairs that are recognized poorly by all the generic systems.

Some approaches consequently propose a component-based model. In this framework, a generic system would have additional special components that take care of special subclasses of entailment pairs. Such a component is involved when a pair of its subclass is recognized. Vanderwende and Dolan (2005), and subsequently Vanderwende et al. (2006), divide all the entailment pairs according to whether categorization could be accurately predicted based solely on syntactic cues. Related to this, Akhmatova and Dras (2007) present an entailment type where the relationship expressed in the Hypothesis is encoded in a syntactic construction in the Text.

Vanderwende et al. (2006) note that what they term *is-a* relationships are a particular problem in their approach. Observing that this encompasses hypernymy relations, and that there has been a fair amount of recent work on hypernymy acquisition, where ontologies containing hypernymy relations are extended with corpus-derived additions, we propose a HYPERNYMY ENTAILMENT TYPE to look at in this paper. In this type, the Hypothesis states a hypernymy relationship between elements of the Text: for example, *This was seen as a betrayal by the EZLN and other political groups* implies that *EZLN is a political group*. This subtype is of particular relevance to Question Answering (QA): in the RTE-2 dataset,[1] for example, all *is-a* Hypotheses were drawn from QA data.

In this paper we take the hypernymy acquisition work of Snow et al. (2005) as a starting point, and then investigate how to adapt it to an entailment context. We see this as an investigation of a more general approach, where work in a separate area of NLP can be adapted to define a related entailment subclass.

Section 2 of the paper discusses the relevant work from the areas of component-based RTE and hypernymy extraction. Section 3 defines the hypernymy entailment type and expands on the main idea of the paper. Section 4 describes the experimental set-up and the results; and Section 5 concludes the work.

## 2 Related Work

### 2.1 Component-based RTE

Vanderwende et al. (2006) use an approach based on logical forms, which they generate by the NLPwin parser. Nodes in the resulting syntactic dependency graphs for Text and Hypothesis are then heuristically aligned; then syntax-based heuristics

[1] http://pascallin.ecs.soton.ac.uk/Challenges/RTE2, (Bar-Haim et al., 2006)



*Proceedings of the 2009 Workshop on Applied Textual Inference, ACL-IJCNLP 2009*, pages 52–60,
Suntec, Singapore, 6 August 2009. 

are applied to detect false entailments. As noted above, *is-a* relations fared particularly badly. In our approach, we do not use such a heavy duty representation for the task, using instead the techniques of hypernym acquisition described in Section 2.2. Cabrio et al. (2008) proposed what they call a combined specialized entailment engine. They have created a general framework, based on distance between T and H (they measure the cost of the editing operations such as insertion, deletion and substitution, which are required to transform the text T into the hypothesis H) and several modular entailment engines, each of which is able to deal with an aspect of language variability such as negation or modal verbs. Akhmatova and Dras (2007) built a specific component from a subset of entailment pairs that are poorly recognized by generic systems participating in an RTE Challenge. These are the entailment pairs where a specific syntactic construction in the Text encodes a semantic relationship between its elements that is explicitly shown in the Hypothesis, as in example (1):

(1) *Text:* Japan's Kyodo news agency said the US could be ready to set up a liaison office—the lowest level of diplomatic representation—in Pyongyang if it abandons its nuclear program.
*Hypothesis:* Kyodo news agency is based in Japan.

The entailment pairs share a set of similar features: they have a very high word overlap regardless of being a *true* or *false* entailments, for example. High word overlap is one of the features for an RTE system for the majority of the entailment pair types, which presumably hints at *true*, but this is not useful in our case. Akhmatova and Dras (2007) described a two-fold probabilistic approach to recognizing entailment, that in its turn was based on the well-known noisy channel model from Statistical Machine Translation (Brown et al., 1990). In the work of this paper, by contrast, we look at only identifying a hypernymy-related Text, so the problem reduces to one of classification over the Text.

## 2.2 Hypernymy Extraction

The aim of work on hypernymy extraction is usually the enrichment of a lexical resource such as WordNet, or creation of specific hierarchical lexical data directly for the purpose of some application, such as information extraction or question answering. There can be found several approaches to the task of hypernymy extraction: co-occurrence approaches, asymmetric association measures, and pattern-based methods.

**Cooccurence Approaches** Co-occurrence approaches first cluster words into similarity classes and consider the elements of a class to be siblings of one parent. Therefore the search for a parent for some members from the class gives a parent for the other members of the class. The first work that introduced co-occurrence methods to the field is that of Caraballo (1999). First she clusters nouns into groups based on conjunctive and appositive data collected from the Wall Street Journal. Nouns are grouped according to the similarity of being seen with other nouns in conjunctive and appositive relationships. In the second stage, using some knowledge about which conjuncts connect hypernyms reliably, a parent for a group of nouns is searched for in the same text corpora. Other co-occurrence methods can be found in works by Pantel et al. (2004) and Pantel and Ravichandran (2004).

**Asymmetric Association Measures** In Asymmetric Association (see Dias et al. (2008)) hypernymy is derived through the measure of how much one word 'attracts' another one. When hearing "fruit", more common fruits will be likely to come into mind such as "apple" or "banana". In this case, there exists an oriented association between "fruit" and "mango" (mango $\rightarrow$ fruit) which indicates that "mango" attracts "fruit" moreso than "fruit" attracts "mango". As a consequence, "fruit" is more likely to be a more general term than "mango".

**Pattern-based Methods** Pattern-based methods are based on the observation that hypernyms tend to be connected in the sentences by specific words or patterns, and that some patterns can predict hypernymy with very high probability, like the *X and other Y* pattern. Generally, some amount of manual work on finding the seed patterns is done first. Automated algorithms use these patterns for discovering more patterns and for the subsequent hypernymy extraction. The fundamental work for the pattern-based approaches is that of Hearst (1992). More recently, Snow et al. (2005) and Snow et al. (2006) have described a method of hypernymy extraction using machine learning of patterns. Pattern-based methods are known to be successfully used for the creation of hierarchical data for other languages as well, such as Dutch; for example, see Tjong Kim Sang and Hofmann (2007). For our purposes, pattern-based methods are particularly suitable, as we have as context two words and a single pattern connecting them; we thus describe these approaches in more detail.

In her early work on pattern-based hypernymy extraction Hearst (1992) noticed that a particular semantic relationship between two nouns in the sentence can be indicated by the presence of certain lexico-syntactic patterns linking those nouns. Hypernymy (*is-a*, *is a kind of* relation) is one such relationship.

Linking two noun phrases via the patterns $such\ NP_y\ as\ NP_x$ often implies that $NP_x$ is a hyponym of $NP_y$, that is $NP_x$ *is a kind of* $NP_y$. She gives the following example to illustrate the patterns

(2) The bow lute, such as the Bambara ndang, is plucked and has an individual curved neck for each string.

Hearst comments that most fluent readers of English who have never before encountered the term *Bambara ndang* will nevertheless from this sentence infer that a *Bambara ndang* is a kind of *bow lute*. This is true even if the reader has only a fuzzy conception of what a bow lute is. The complete set of patterns semi-automatically found by Hearst are:

1. $NP_y\ and\ other\ NP_x$
2. $NP_y\ or\ other\ NP_x$
3. $NP_y\ such\ as\ NP_x$
4. $such\ NP_y\ as\ NP_x$
5. $NP_y\ including\ NP_x$
6. $NP_y,\ especially\ NP_x$

Snow et al. (2005) had the aim of building upon Hearst's work in order to extend the WordNet semantic taxonomy by adding to it hypernym-hyponym pairs of nouns that are connected by a wider set of lexico-syntactic pairs. They developed an automatic approach for finding hypernym-hyponym pairs of nouns in the text corpus without a set of predefined patterns.

The work was carried out on a corpus of 6 million newswire sentences. Every pair of nouns $(n_i, n_j)$ in the sentence was extracted. The pairs were labelled as Known Hypernym pair if $n_j$ is an ancestor of the first sense of $n_i$ in the WordNet hypernym taxonomy (Fellbaum, 1998). A noun pair might have been assigned to the second set of Known Non-Hypernym pairs if both nouns are contained within WordNet, but neither noun is an ancestor of the other in the WordNet hypernym taxonomy for any senses of either noun. Each sentence was parsed using MINIPAR. The dependency relations between $n_i$ and $n_j$ constituted the lexico-syntactic patterns connecting Known Hypernyms or Known Non-Hypernyms. The main idea of their work was then to collect all the lexico-syntactic patterns that may indicate the hypernymy relation and use them as the features for a decision tree to classify NP pairs as hypernym-hyponym or not-hypernym-hyponym pairs.

Snow et al. (2005) state in their work that the dependency paths acquired automatically contained all the patterns mentioned in Hearst (1992). The comparison of the results of a classifier whose vectors were created from all the patterns seen with the Known Hypernyms in their corpus, and a classifier whose vectors contained only the patterns of Hearst (1992), showed that the results of the former classifier are considerably better than that of the latter one. In an RTE context where the entailment recognition relies on recognising hypernymy, an approach like this, where patterns acquired from a corpus are used, could be useful; but how it should best be adapted is not clear. That is then the goal of this paper.

## 3 Hypernymy Entailment Type

### 3.1 Definition

We define *Hypernymy Entailment* to be an entailment relationship where the *is-a* relationship between two nouns in the hypothesis is 'hidden behind' the lexico-syntactic pattern connecting them in the text. Being more precise, the Text-Hypothesis pairs of interest have the following characteristics:

1. The Hypothesis is a simple sentence. That is a sentence that consists of a subject, a 3rd person form the verb *to be*, and a direct object, and that contains no subordinate clauses.

2. Both subject and object of the Hypothesis (or in some cases their morphological variants) are found in the text.

Thus, the hypernymy relationship is not stated in the Text, but is hidden in the way the subject and object of the Hypothesis are connected to each other in the Text. Examples of the *true* hypernymy entailment pairs are as follows:[2]

(3) *Text:* Soon after the EZLN had returned to Chiapas, Congress approved a different version of the COCOPA Law, which did not include the autonomy clauses, claiming they were in contradiction with some constitutional rights (private property and secret voting); this was seen as a betrayal by the EZLN and other political groups.
*Hypothesis:* EZLN is a political group.

Both *EZLN* and *political groups* are present in the text sentence, and are connected by an *is-a* relation in the hypothesis. The pattern *and other* and the syntactical connection between the noun phrases give a good indication that the noun phrases are in the hypernym-hyponym relationship. An example of a *false* hypernymy entailment pair is as follows:

(4) *Text:* Laboring side by side on the outer hull of the station's crew quarters, Vladimir Dezhurov and Mikhail Turin mounted science packages and two Eastman Kodak Co. placards while U.S. astronaut Frank Culbertson looked on from inside the complex.
*Hypothesis:* Vladimir Dezhurov is a U.S. astronaut.

### 3.2 Idea

In the case of Snow et al. (2005) the main accent is on automatic extraction of all the patterns that might, even if not reliably on their own, predict the hypernymy relation between two nouns. Their task is, given a previously unseen pair of nouns, to determine whether they are in a hypernymy relationship, using a classifier whose feature values are derived from many occurrences of acquired patterns in a corpus.

In our own work we are put in the situation where there is only one pattern that is available to judge if two words are in a hypernym/hyponym relation, not the whole text corpus as in the case of Snow et al. (2005). Thus, we are mostly interested in the prediction of the hypernymy using this pattern that is available for us. The fact that the named entities we are working with, such as person, organization, location, are not that frequently seen in any text corpora also shifts the accent onto the pattern rather than on the word pair itself. As well as the fact that even in the case when two words are hypernym-hyponym, that may not follow at all from the sentence that they are seen in; and non hypernym-hyponym pair can be used as such in a metaphoric expression or just in a particular sentence we are dealing with. To illustrate, consider example (5):

(5) *Text:* Note that the auxiliary verb function derives from the copular function; and, depending on one's point of view, one can still interpret the verb *as a* copula and the following verbal form as being adjectival.
*Hypothesis:* A copular is a verb.

Snow et al. (2005) aim to determine whether *copular* and *verb* are in a hypernymy relation; to this end they use the *as a* pattern as in this example, along with all others throughout the corpus. The reliability of the *as a* pattern (which as it turns out is quite high) adds weight to the accumulated evidence, but is not the sole evidence. In the individual case, however, it can be incorrect, as in example (6):

(6) *Text:* In the 1980s, Minneapolis took its place *as a* center of the arts, with the Walker Arts Center leading the nation in appreciation of pop and postmodern art , and a diverse range of musicians, from Prince to Hüsker Dü to the Replacements to the Suburbs to Soul Asylum keeping up with the nation in musical innovation.
*Hypothesis:* A centre is a place.

Example (6) has a similar structure to example (5), but *center* governs a preposition *of* after it, that seem to make the hypernymy more doubtful in this context. Taking into account all of the above, the major focus of the work has shifted for us from the word pair to the environment it has occurred in. Thus, we use the major ideas from the work of Snow et al. (2005), but as we show below, it is necessary to develop a more complex set of counts in order to apply this to our entailments type. In particular, we expect that the division of patterns into lexical and syntactic parts, in order to score them separately, is beneficial for entailment. Again, it is a result of scarcity of information: we have only one text sentence, not the whole text corpus to make the entailment decision.

[2]Examples (3) - (4) are taken from the RTE2 test corpus.

## 4 Experimental Setup

### 4.1 Data

Our goal is to build a classifier that will detect whether a given potential hypernymy entailment pair is true or false; we first need to construct sets of such pairs for training and testing. As our basic data source, we use 500 000 sentences from the Wikipedia XML corpus (Denoyer and Gallinari, 2006); this is the corpus used by Akhmatova and Dras (2007), and related to one used in one set of experiments by Snow et al. (2005). These sentences were parsed with the MINIPAR parser.

We identified Known Hypernym pairs as did Snow et al. (2005) (see Section 2.2); of our basic corpus, 13310 sentences contained Known Hypernyms. From these sentences we extracted the dependency relations between the Known Hypernyms, of which there were 166 different types; we refer to these as syntactic patterns hereafter.

We reserved 259 of these sentences to construct a test set for our approach, as described below. These sentences were selected randomly in proportion to the syntactic patterns occurring in the overall set. The remaining sentences constituted our SYNTACTIC PATTERN TRAINING SET. For the test set, these sentences constituted the Texts; to derive the Hypotheses, we extracted the Known Hypernyms and connected them by *is a*. These sentences were annotated with *yes* if they entail hypernymy, and *no* otherwise; the resulting annotated data has 2:1 ratio of *no* to *yes*. The main annotation was carried out by the first author, with the second author carrying out a separate annotation to evaluate agreement. The number of items where there was agreement was 206, giving a $\kappa$ of 0.54. This is broadly in line with the $\kappa$ found in construction of the RTE datasets ($\kappa = 0.6$) (Glickman, 2006) where it is characterized as "moderate agreement", based on Landis and Koch (1977). Results later are presented for both the overall set of 259 (based on the first author's original annotations) and for the subset with agreement of 206.

As our additional, much larger data source for deriving purely lexical patterns and associated scores, we use the Web1T n-gram corpus (Brants and Franz, 2006), which provides n-grams and their counts for up to 5-grams inclusive. We use these n-grams to get the lexical patterns of length 1, 2 and 3 that connect Known Hypernyms and Known Non-Hypernyms correspondingly. The length is up to 3 as we need 2 slots for the nouns from the pair itself. The counts are extracted with the help of the software *get1t* written by Hawker et al. (2007). We refer to this as our LEXICAL PATTERN TRAINING SET.

### 4.2 Baselines

We use two baselines. The first is a simple most-frequent one, choosing always false (noting from Section 4.1 that this is more common by a ratio of approximately 2:1). For the second one, we attempt to use the idea of Snow et al. (2005) in a straightforward way. We note again that the fixed context for a given Known Hypernym pair that we have, unlike Snow et al. (2005), is the single Text; we therefore cannot apply the classifier from that work directly. Our second baseline based on their approach is as follows. For each sentence we look at all nouns it contains. If a pair of nouns from the sentence is a Known-Hypernym pair we save the lexical pattern connecting the nouns and the syntactic pattern between the nouns in a pattern list. We take into account only those syntactic patterns that have been seen in the corpus at least three times. We then consider that a test entailment pair is a true entailment if both the lexical pattern between the nouns in question and the syntactic connection between them is found in the list.

### 4.3 Two-Part Model

We now propose a two-component model to compensate for the fixed context. The first component, $score_{lex}$, involves the use of the lexical pattern to predict hypernymy. Unless we know something else about the structure of the text sentence, the pattern (a sequence of words) that connects two entities in question is the only evidence of the possible hypernym-hyponym relation between them. It does not guarantee the relation itself, but the more probable it is that the pattern predicts hypernymy, the more probable it is that the entailment relation between the Text and Hypothesis holds. To motivate the second component, we take as an example the pattern $NP_y$ $and$ $other$ $NP_x$, the first of the Hearst (1992) patterns and a good predictor of hypernymy, and consider the following examples:

(7) *Text:* Mr. Smith and other employees stayed in the office.
*Hypothesis:* Mr. Smith is an employee.

(8) *Text:* I talked to Mr. Smith and other

employees stayed in the office.
*Hypothesis:* Mr. Smith is an employee.

*Mr. Smith* and *an employee* are connected in both cases by *and other*. We know that the pattern *and other* is a good indicator of the hypernymy relation. The probability of the pattern *and other* to predict the hypernymy relation is the prior probability of the entailment relation in a text-hypothesis pair. As can be seen in examples (7) and (8), there is an entailment relationship only in example (7); in example (8) entailment does not hold.

The second component $score_{synt}$ is an indicator of the syntactic possibility of the entailment relationship. Hypernym-hyponyms tend to be in certain syntactic relations in the sentence, such as being subjects of the same verb, for example, in the cases where we can decide on the relation of the hypernymy between them. Other syntactic relationships, even though they may connect hypernym and hyponym, do not allow us to conclude that there is a hypernymy relation between the words. As it can be seen from examples (7) and (8), every syntactical relation has its own level of certainty about the hypernym relation between *Mr. Smith* and *an employee*, and therefore about the fact that the Text entails the Hypothesis.

### 4.3.1 Lexical Patterns

From our lexical pattern training corpus, we derived for both Known Hypernym and Known Non-Hypernym pairs, the counts of both tokens (total number of pairs connected) and types (number of different pairs connected). To illustrate, we take two example pairs, $w_1 = rock$ and $w_2 = material$, and $w_1 = rice$ and $w_2 = grain$. We find *rock , and other material* occurs 47 times, and *rice , and other grain* 166 times. Totalling these, that would give us the following statistics for the pattern *, and other*: seen with the Known Hypernyms 213 times (total of tokens), connecting 2 different pairs (total of types). We hypothesize that knowing the number of different types of patterns will be important as a way of compensating for the more limited context relative to Snow et al. (2005) which used only the number of pattern tokens.

The above can be illustrated by the counts obtained for patterns of Hearst (1992); see the first five rows of Table 1. One can see from the first three examples that in all cases the number of times the pattern has been seen with Known Hypernyms is overwhelmingly higher than with that of Known Non-Hypernyms. Even more extremely, in the next two examples in Table 1, Known Non-Hypernyms were not seen with these patterns at all. We contrast these with the non-Hearst patterns (extracted from our lexical pattern corpus) in the last two rows. As one can see, the patterns *and detailed travel* and *online game caribbean* have been seen only with the Known Hypernyms, and the frequency counts are very close to that of the pattern *, especially*. Both patterns however have connected the constituents of only one Known Hypernyms pair. That puts some doubt on the general reliability of the pattern to make hypernymy judgements.

We then define our scoring metric, based on the following quantities: $C(h\text{-}tok)$, the number of times the pattern has been seen with Known Hypernyms; $C(nh\text{-}tok)$, the number of times the pattern has been seen with Known Non-Hypernyms; $C(h\text{-}type)$, the number of times the pattern has been seen with different Known Hypernym patterns; $C(nh\text{-}type)$, the number of times the pattern has been seen with different Known Non-Hypernym patterns. We then define our lexical scoring function as follows:

$$score_{lex} = \frac{C(h\text{-}tok)}{C(h\text{-}tok) + C(nh\text{-}tok)} \times \frac{C(h\text{-}type)}{C(h\text{-}type) + C(nh\text{-}type)}$$

We use it to score patterns where the number of times the pattern has been seen with different Known Hypernyms ($C(h\text{-}type)$) is greater than a threshold, here 5; for patterns below this threshold, the score is 0. We determined on this scoring function in comparison to others (notably using only token proportions, the first term in the scoring function above) by using them to rank patterns and then assess the relative ranking of the Hearst patterns among all others. Under the scoring function above, the Hearst patterns were ranked highest, with patterns *or other, such as* and *and other* taking the first, second and third positions respectively.

### 4.3.2 Syntactic Patterns

To estimate the probability of various syntactic patterns from our syntactic pattern training corpus, ideally we would annotate every sentence as

Table 1: Counts for the patterns of Hearst (1992) obtained from *the Web1T corpus*

| Pattern | seen with | | | |
|---|---|---|---|---|
| | Hypernyms | Non-Hypernyms | Different Hypernyms | Different Non-Hypernyms |
| $NP_y$ and other $NP_x$ | 172036 | 1716 | 486 | 3 |
| $NP_y$ or other $NP_x$ | 421083 | 1016 | 965 | 11 |
| $NP_y$ such as $NP_x$ | 86158 | 384 | 355 | 4 |
| $NP_y$ including $NP_x$ | 68098 | 0 | 251 | 0 |
| $NP_y$, especially $NP_y$ | 10236 | 0 | 80 | 0 |
| $NP_y$ and detailed travel $NP_x$ | 9870 | 0 | 1 | 0 |
| $NP_y$ online game caribbean $NP_x$ | 9874 | 0 | 1 | 0 |

*true* or *false* according to whether the hypernymy is entailed from the sentence or not. The annotation would allow the calculation of the likelihood for every syntactical relation to indicate the entailment relationship.

It is quite a time-consuming task to annotate enough data to get reliable counts for all the syntactical patterns. Therefore, as an approximate first step we have divided all the sentences into three groups according to the type of a lexical patterns that connects a pair of Known Hypernyms: Hearst patterns; the patterns that were found from our lexical pattern training corpus; and all other patterns. We have assumed that Hearst patterns, as being a good indication of hypernymy, may in most cases predict entailment as well; the automatically derived lexical patterns may still sometime predict entailment, but less well than the Hearst patterns; and the unknown patterns are not considered to be good predictors of the entailment at all. Thus, for the initial estimate of the syntactical probabilities of the entailment we have employed a very coarse approximation of the maximum likelihood estimate of the probability of a syntactic pattern implying an entailment, weighting these three groups with the values 1, 0.5 and 0 respectively. This leads to a score as follows:

$$score_{\textit{synt-basic}} = 0.5 \times \frac{C(automatic\ lexical\ pattern)}{C(all\ patterns)} + 1.0 \times \frac{C(Hearst\ pattern)}{C(all\ patterns)}$$

where $C(X)$ represents the count of occurrences of the pattern type $X$.

As a more refined scoring metric, we identified the set of the most frequent syntactic patterns and annotated data for them, in order to improve their probability estimates. Taking the seven most frequent, we annotated 100 randomly chosen sentences for each of the syntactical patterns containing them from the syntactic pattern training corpus. As a result of the annotation the probabilities of the syntactical patterns to indicate entailment has changed. The basic probabilities and the revised probabilities for these seven syntactic patterns can be found in Table 2.

Table 2: Syntactic Pattern Probabilities

| **Pattern** | **Basic P** | **Improved P** |
|---|---|---|
| obj | 0.34 | 0.0 |
| pcomp-n_ mod | 0.40 | 0.038 |
| appo | 0.73 | 0.90 |
| conj | 0.76 | 0.10 |
| mod_ pcomp-n | 0.64 | 0.38 |
| mod_ pcomp-n_ mod | 0.45 | 0.023 |
| mod_ conj | 0.97 | 0.10 |

Table 3: Model Evaluation (full set of 259 / agreed subset of 206)

| **Model** | **Accuracy** |
|---|---|
| Baseline (most frequent) | 69% / 70% |
| Baseline (Snow) | 71% / 72% |
| Lexical component only | 60% / 60% |
| Improved syntactic component only | 67% / 69% |
| Lexical and Basic Syntactic Component | 76% / 73% |
| Lexical and Improved Syntactic Component | 82% / 83% |

### 4.4 Results and Discussion

We combine the lexical and syntactic scores as features to the J48 decision tree of WEKA (Witten and Frank, 1999). Our evaluation is a 10-fold cross-validation on the test set. Results are as in Table 3, presented for both the full test set of 259 and for the subset with agreement of 206.

We note first of all that the simple approach derived from Snow et al. (2005), as described in Section 4.2, does perform marginally better than the baseline of choosing always false. The lexical or syntactic components alone do not perform better than the most-frequent baseline approach. This is expected, as that approach includes both lexical and syntactic components. The lexical combined with the basic syntactic component does improve over the baselines. However, the lexical combined with the improved syntactic component experiences a much higher improvement. Overall, the results for the full set and for the subset are broadly the same, showing the same relative behaviour.

The lexical only component falsely recognizes examples such as example (9) as true, as it has no support of syntax. Just a comma by itself sufficiently frequently indicates entailment in case of apposition, so the lexical component is misled.

(9) *Text:* There were occasional outbreaks of violence, but most observers considered it remarkable that such an obvious breakdown of the capitalist system had not led to a rapid growth of socialism, communism, or fascism (as happened for example in Germany).
*Hypothesis:* Communism is a socialism.

Syntax only, even though it prevents the mistakes of the lexical-only component for the examples above, introduces its own mistakes. Knowing that the subject and object in the Hypothesis are linked by direct dependency relations to a preposition in the Text is useful, but without a lexical pattern can be too permissive, as in example (10):

(10) *Text:* However, Griffin attracted criticism for writing in the aftermath of the bombing of the Admiral Duncan pub bombing (which killed three people, including a pregnant woman) that the gay people protesting against the murders were "flaunting their perversion in front of the world's journalists, and showed just why so many ordinary people find these creatures disgusting".
*Hypothesis:* Criticism is a writing.

Both baseline and the final hypernymy entailment engine work well in the cases where the counts for or against entailment are very high, as in examples (11) and (12), which are correctly recognized as a true and a false entailment by both systems.

(11) *Text:* Carbon compounds form the basis of all life on Earth and the carbon-nitrogen cycle provides some of the energy produced by the sun and other stars.
*Hypothesis:* Sun is a star.

(12) *Text:* In 1792 British explorer George Vancouver set up a small settlement near the village of Yerba Buena (later downtown San Francisco) which became a small base for English, Russian, and other European fur traders, explorers, and settlers.
*Hypothesis:* Village is a settlement.

The final hypernymy system works better for more marginal cases, such as example (13).

(13) *Text:* The trials were held in the German city of Nuremberg from 1945 to 1949 at the Nuremberg Palace of Justice.
*Hypothesis:* Nuremberg is a city.

The pattern *of* can not be called a good hint for hypernymy, but in some special cases, like that of the city and its name, the hypernymy is obvious. Division into lexical and syntactic parts helped in discovering the pattern and adjusting better its probability of entailing hypernymy. All this supports our idea that to compensate for the lack of information in the case of RTE the lexico-syntactic patterns should be divided into their lexical and syntactic components.

## 5 Conclusion

In this paper we have shown how work in hypernymy acquisition can be adapted to tackle a specific subtype of related entailment problem. Following work by Snow et al. (2005), we have defined an obvious first adaptation which nonetheless marginally improves over the baseline. We have then shown that by separating lexical and syntactic patterns we can obtain a significant improvement on the entailment classification accuracy. In our future work we aim to construct a baseline generic RTE engine and test its performance with and without this and other components in order to analyse the work of a component-based model as a whole. The approach also suggests that adapting work from other areas of NLP for entailment subclasses is promising.

## References


Elena Akhmatova and Mark Dras. 2007. Entailment due to syntactically encoded semantic relationships. In *Proceedings of ALTA-2007*, pages 4–12.

Roy Bar-Haim, Ido Dagan, Bill Dolan, Lisa Ferro, Danilo Giampiccolo, Bernardo Magnini, and Idan Szpektor. 2006. The second pascal recognising textual entailment challenge. In *The second PASCAL Recognising Textual Entailment Challenge*, pages 3–11, Venice, Italy.

Thorsten Brants and Alex Franz. 2006. Web 1t 5-gram corpus version 1. Technical report, Google Research.

Peter F. Brown, John Cocke, Stephen A. Della Pietra, Vincent J. Della Pietra, Fredrick Jelinek, John D. Lafferty, Robert L. Mercer, and Paul S. Roossin. 1990. A statistical approach to machine translation. In *Computational Linguistics*, volume 16, pages 79 – 85.

Elena Cabrio, Milen Kouylekov, and Bernardo Magnini. 2008. Combining specialized entailment engines for RTE-4. In *Proceedings of TAC-2008*.

Sharon Caraballo. 1999. Automatic acquisition of a hypernym-labeled noun hierarchy from text. In *Proceedings of ACL-99*, pages 120–126.

Ido Dagan, Oren Glickman, and Bernardo Magnini. 2006. The pascal recognising textual entailment challenge. In *Quionero-Candela, J.; Dagan, I.; Magnini, B.; d'Alch-Buc, F. (Eds.) Machine Learning Challenges. Lecture Notes in ComputerScience*, volume 3944, pages 177 – 190. Springer.

Ludovic Denoyer and Patrick Gallinari. 2006. The Wikipedia XML Corpus. In *SIGIR Forum, 40(1)*, pages 64–69.

Gaël Dias, Raycho Mukelov, and Guillaume Cleuziou. 2008. Unsupervised learning of general-specific noun relations from the web. In *Proceedings of FLAIRS Conference*, pages 147–152.

Christiane Fellbaum. 1998. *WordNet: An Electronic Lexical Database*. The MIT Press.

Oren Glickman. 2006. *Applied Textual Entailment*. Ph.D. thesis, Bar Ilan University.

Tobias Hawker, Mary Gardiner, and Andrew Bennetts. 2007. Practical queries of a massive n-gram database. In *Proceedings of ALTA-2007*, pages 40–48.

Marti A. Hearst. 1992. Automatic acquisition of hyponyms from large text corpora. In *COLING*, pages 539–545.

Richard J. Landis and Gary G. Koch. 1977. The measurement of observer agreement for categorical data. *Biometrics*, 33(1):159–174.

Patrick Pantel and Deepak Ravichandran. 2004. Automatically labeling semantic classes. In *Proceedings of HLT/NAACL-04*, pages 321–328.

Patrick Pantel, Deepak Ravichandran, and Eduard Hovy. 2004. Towards terascale semantic acquisition. In *Proceedings of Coling 2004*, pages 771–777, Geneva, Switzerland, Aug 23–Aug 27.

Rion Snow, Daniel Jurafsky, and Andrew Y. Ng. 2005. Learning syntactic patterns for automatic hypernym discovery. In Lawrence K. Saul, Yair Weiss, and Léon Bottou, editors, *Advances in Neural Information Processing Systems 17*, pages 1297–1304, Cambridge, MA. MIT Press.

Rion Snow, Daniel Jurafsky, and Andrew Y. Ng. 2006. Semantic taxonomy induction from heterogenous evidence. In *Proceedings of ACL-2006*, pages 801–808.

E.F. Tjong Kim Sang and K. Hofmann. 2007. Automatic extraction of dutch hypernym-hyponym pairs. In *Proceedings of CLIN-2006*, Leuven, Belgium. LOT, Netherlands Graduate School of Linguistics.

Lucy Vanderwende and William B. Dolan. 2005. What syntax can contribute in the entailment task. In *Proceedings of MLCW*, pages 205–216.

Lucy Vanderwende, Arul Menezes, and Rion Snow. 2006. Microsoft research at RTE-2: Syntactic contributions in the entailment task: an implementation. In *Proceedings of 2nd PASCAL Challenges Workshop on Recognizing Textual Entailment*.

Ian H. Witten and Eibe Frank. 1999. *Data Mining: Practical Machine Learning Tools and Techniques with Java Implementations*. Morgan Kaufmann.

# Automating Model Building in c-rater

**Jana Z. Sukkarieh**
Educational Testing Service
Rosedale Road, Princeton, NJ 08541
jsukkarieh@ets.org

**Svetlana Stoyanchev**
Stony Brook University
Stony Brook, NY, 11794
svetastenchikova@gmail.com

## Abstract

c-rater is Educational Testing Service's technology for the content scoring of short student responses. A major step in the scoring process is Model Building where variants of model answers are generated that correspond to the rubric for each item or test question. Until recently, Model Building was knowledge-engineered (KE) and hence labor and time intensive. In this paper, we describe our approach to automating Model Building in c-rater. We show that c-rater achieves comparable accuracy on automatically built and KE models.

## 1 Introduction

c-rater (Leacock and Chodorow, 2003) is Educational Testing Service's (ETS) technology for the automatic content scoring of short free-text student answers, ranging in length from a few words to approximately 100 words. While other content scoring systems [e.g., Intelligent. Essay Assessor (Foltz, Laham and Landauer, 2003), SEAR (Christie, 1999), IntelliMetric (Vantage Learning Tech, 2000)] take a holistic[1] approach, c-rater takes an analytical approach to scoring content. The item rubrics specify content in terms of main points or concepts required to appear in a student's correct answer. An example of a test question or item follows:

| | |
|---|---|
| **Item 1 (Full credit: 2 points)**<br>*Stimulus:* A Reading passage<br><br>*Prompt:*<br>In the space below, write the question that Alice was most likely trying to answer when she performed Step *B*. | *Concepts or main/key points:*<br>**$C_1$:** How does rain formation occur in winter?<br>**$C_2$:** How is rain formed?<br>**$C_3$:** How do temperature and altitude contribute to the formation of rain? |
| *Scoring rules:*<br>2 points for C1<br>1 for C2 (only if C1 is not present)<br>1 for C3 (only if C1 and C2 are not present)<br>Otherwise 0 | |

We view c-rater's task as a **textual entailment (TE)** problem. We use TE here to mean either a paraphrase or an inference (up to the context of the item or test question). c-rater's task is reduced to a TE problem in the following way:

> **Given** a concept, *C*, (e.g., "body increases its temperature") **and** a student answer, *A*, (e.g., either "the body raises temperature," "the body responded. His temperature was 37° and now it is 38°," or "Max has a fever") **and** the context of the item, **the goal is** to check whether *C* is an inference or paraphrase of *A* (in other words, *A* implies *C* and *A* is true).

There are four main steps in c-rater. The first one is **Model Building (MB)**, where a set of model answers are generated (either manually or automatically). Second, c-rater automatically processes model answers and students' answers using a set of natural language processing (NLP) tools and extracts the linguistic features. Third, the matching algorithm **Goldmap** uses the linguistic features culminated from both MB and NLP to automatically determine whether a student's response entails the expected concepts. Finally, c-rater applies

[1] Holistic means an overall score is given for a student's answer as opposed to scores for individual components of a student's answer.



*Proceedings of the 2009 Workshop on Applied Textual Inference, ACL-IJCNLP 2009*, pages 61–69, Suntec, Singapore, 6 August 2009. 

the scoring rules to produce a score and feedback that justifies the score to the student.

Until recently, MB was knowledge-engineered (KE). The KE approach for one item required, on average, 12 hours of time and labor. This paper describes our approach to automatic MB. We show that c-rater achieves comparable accuracy on automatically- and manually-built models. Section 2 outlines others' work in this domain and emphasizes the contribution of this paper. Section 3 outlines c-rater. In Section 4, we describe how MB works. Section 5 explains how we automate the process. Prior to the conclusion, we report the evaluation of this work.

## 2 Automatic Content Scoring: Others' Work

A few systems that deal with both **short answers** and **analytic-based** content exist. The task, in general, is reduced to comparing a student's answer to a model answer. Recent work by Mohler and Mihalcea (2009) at the University of North Texas uses unsupervised methods in text-to-text semantic similarity comparing unseen students' answers to one correct answer. Previous work, including c-rater, used supervised techniques to compare unseen students' answers to the space of potentially "all possible correct answers" specified in the rubric of the item at hand. The techniques varied from information extraction with knowledge-engineered patterns representing the model answers [Automark at Intelligent Assessment Technologies (Mitchell, 2002), the Oxford-UCLES system (Sukkarieh, et. al., 2003) at the University of Oxford] to data mining techniques using very shallow linguistic features [e.g., Sukkarieh and Pulman (2005) and CarmelTC at Carnegie Mellon University (Rose, et al. 2003)]. Data mining techniques proved not to be very transparent when digging up justifications for scores.

c-rater's model building process is similar to generating patterns but the patterns in c-rater are written in English instead of a formal language. The aim of the process is to produce a non-trivial space of possible correct answers guided by a subset of the students' answers. The motivation is that the best place to look for variations and refinements for the rubric is the students' answers. This is what test developers do before piloting a large-scale exam. From an NLP point of view, the idea is that generating this space will make scoring an unseen answer easier than just having one correct answer. However, similar to what other systems reported, generating manually-engineered patterns is very costly. In Sukkarieh et al. (2004) there was an attempt to generate patterns automatically but the results reported were not comparable to those using manually-generated patterns. This paper presents improvements on previous supervised approaches by automating the process of model-answer building using well-known NLP methods and resources while yielding comparable results to knowledge-engineered methods.

## 3 c-rater, in Brief

In c-rater, manual MB has its own graphical interface, **Alchemist**. MB uses the NLP tools and **Goldmap** (which reside in the **c-rater Engine**). On the other hand, Goldmap depends on the model generated. The c-rater Engine performs NLP on input text and concept recognition or TE between the input text and each concept (see Figure 1). First, a student answer is processed for **spelling corrections** in an attempt to decrease the noise for subsequent NLP tools. In the next stage, **parts-of-speech tagging** and **parsing** are performed (the OpenNLP parser is used http://opennlp.sourceforge.net). In the third stage, a parse tree is passed through a **feature extractor**. Manually-generated rules extract features from the parse tree. The result is a flat structure representing phrases, predicates, and relationships between predicates and entities. Each phrase is annotated with a label indicating whether it is independent or dependent. Each entity is annotated with a syntactic and semantic role. In the **pronoun resolution** stage, pronouns are resolved to either an entity in the student's answer or the question. Finally, a **morphology analyzer** reduces words to their lemmas.[2] The culmination of the above tools results in a set of linguistic features used by the matching algorithm, Goldmap. In addition to the item-independent linguistic features collected by the NLP tools, Goldmap uses item-dependent features specified in MB to decide whether a student's answer, *A*, and a model

[2] We do not go into detail, assuming that the reader is familiar with the described NLP techniques.

answer match, i.e. that concept *C* represented in the model answer, is entailed by *A*.

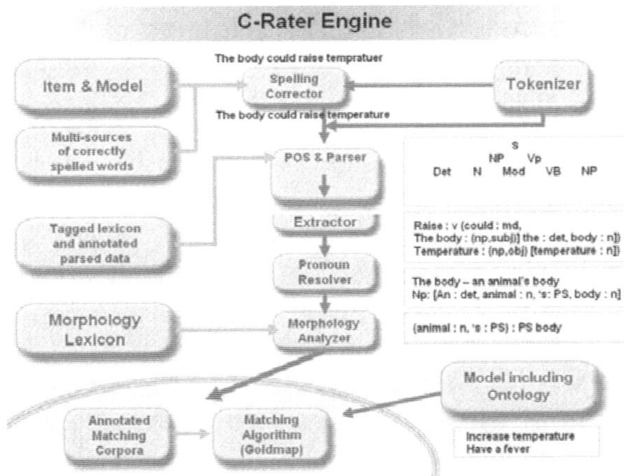


**Figure 1.** c-rater Engine

## 4 KE Model Building

A dataset of student answers for an item is split into development (DEV), cross-validation (XVAL), and blind (BLIND) datasets. DEV is used to build the model, XVAL is used to validate it and BLIND is used to evaluate it. All datasets are double-scored holistically by human raters and the scoring process takes an average 3 hours per item for a dataset of roughly 200 answers.

For each concept $C_i$ in item *X*, a model builder uses DEV to create a set of ***Model Sentences*** ($MS_{ij}$) that s/he believes entails concept $C_i$ in the context of the item. S/he is required to write $MS_{ij}$ in complete sentences. For each model sentence $MS_{ij}$, the model builder selects the ***Required Lexicon*** ($RL_{ijk}$), a set of the most essential lexical entities required to appear in a student's answer. Then, for each $RL_{ijk}$, the model builder selects a set of ***Similar Lexicon*** ($SL_{ijkt}$), guided by the list of words automatically extracted from a dependency-based thesaurus (cs.ualberta.ca/~lindek/downloads.htm).

The process is exemplified in Figure 2. Presented with the concept, *"What causes rain to form in winter time?,"* a model builder writes model sentences like *"Why does rain fall in the winter?,"* highlights or selects lexical items that s/he believes are the required tokens (e.g., *"why," "rain," "fall," "in," "winter"*) and writes a list of similar lexical entities for each required token if needed (e.g., *{descend, go~down, …}* are similar to words like *"fall"*).[3]

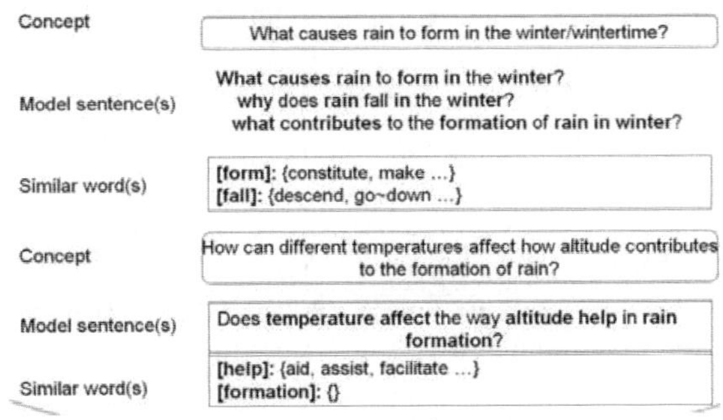


**Figure 2**. KE Model Building

The model for each item *X* is comprised of the scoring rules**,** the collections of model sentences $MS_{ij}$, associated lexical entities $RL_{ijk}$, and corresponding similar lexicon $SL_{ijkt}$. Each model answer is written in terms of $MS_{ij}$ where:

> $MS_{ij}$ entails $C_i$ for $i=1,\ldots, N$, and *N* is the number of concepts specified for item *X*. For each concept $C_i$, Goldmap checks whether answer *A* entails $C_i$, by checking whether *A* entails one of the model sentences $MS_{ij}$, given the additional features $RL_{ijk}$ and corresponding $SL_{ijkt}$.

In practice, model building works as follows. The model builder, guided by the DEV dataset and holistic scores, starts with writing a few model sentences and selects corresponding required ($RL_{ijk}$) and similar ($SL_{ijkt}$) lexicon. S/he then uses the **c-rater engine** to automatically evaluate the model using the DEV dataset, i.e., using the model produced up to that point. Goldmap is used to detect if any answers in the DEV dataset contain any of the model sentences and scores are assigned for each answer. If the scoring agreement between c-rater and each of the two human raters (in terms of a kappa statistic) is much lower than that between the two human raters, then the model is judged unsuitable and the process continues iteratively until kappa statistics on the DEV dataset are satisfactory, i.e., c-rater's agreement with human raters is as high as the kappa between human raters. Once kappa statistics on DEV are satisfactory, the model builder uses

[3] We use lexicon, lexical entities, words, terms and tokens interchangeably meaning either uni- or bi-grams.

c-rater to evaluate the model on the XVAL dataset automatically. Again, until the scoring agreement between c-rater and human raters on XVAL dataset is satisfactory, the model builder iteratively changes the model. Unlike the DEV dataset, the XVAL dataset is never seen by a model builder. The logic here is that over-fitting DEV is a concern, making it hard or impossible to generalize beyond this set. Hence, the results on XVAL can help prevent over-fitting and ideally would predict results over unseen data.

Note that a model builder can introduce what we call a negative concept $C_i^{-1}$ for a concept $C_i$ and adjust the scoring rules accordingly. When this happens, a model builder writes model sentences $MS_i^{-1}{}_j$ entailing $C_i^{-1}$, and selects required words $RL_i^{-1}{}_{jk}$ and corresponding similar words $SL_i^{-1}{}_{jkt}$ in the same way for any other (positive) concept.

On average, MB takes 12 hours of manual work per item (plus 2 hours, on average, for an optional model review by someone other than the model builder). This process is time consuming and error-prone despite utilizing a user-friendly interface like Alchemist. In addition, the satisfaction criterion while building a model is subjective to the model builder.

## 5 Automated Model Building

The process of writing model sentences described above involves: 1) finding the parts of students' answers containing the concept for each expected concept, 2) abstracting over "similar" parts, and 3) representing the abstraction in one (or more) model sentence(s). The process, as mentioned earlier, is similar to writing rules for information extraction, but here one writes them in English sentences and not in a formal language. In practice, there is no mechanism in Alchemist to cluster "similar" parts and MB, in this aspect, is not performed in any systematic manner. Hence, we introduce what we call **concept-based scoring** – used instead of the holistic human scoring. In concept-based scoring, human raters annotate students' responses for each concept *C*, and highlight the part of the answer that entails *C*. In Sukkarieh and Blackmore (2009), we describe concept-based scoring in detail and how this helps in the KE-MB approach. In this paper, we extend the approach by showing how concept-based scores used in the automated approach reduce the time needed for MB substantially while yielding comparable results. Concept-based scoring is done manually. On average, it takes around 3.5 hours per item for a dataset of roughly 200 answers.

The MB process is reduced to:

1. Concept-based scoring
2. Automatically selecting required lexicon
3. Automatically selecting similar lexicon

While holistic scoring takes on average 3 hours for a dataset of 200 answers, concept-based scoring takes 3.5 hours for the same set. However, automated MB takes 0 hours of human intervention–a substantial reduction over the 12 hours required for manual MB.

### 5.1 Concept-based Scoring

We have developed a concept-based scoring interface (CBS) that can be customized for each item [due to lack of space we do not include an illustration]. The CBS interface displays a student's answer to an item and all of the concepts corresponding to that item. The terms *{Absent, Present, Negated}* are what we call analytic or concept-based scores. Using CBS, the human scorer clicks *Present* when a concept is present and *Negated* when a concept is negated or refuted (the default is *Absent*). This is done for each concept. The human scorer also highlights the part of a student's answer that entails the concept in the context of the item. We call a quote corresponding to concept *C* 'Positive Evidence' or 'Negative Evidence' for *Present* and *Negated*, respectively. For example, assume a student answer for Item 1 is *"Her research tells us a lot about rain and hail; in particular, the impact that temperature variations have on altitude contribute to the formation of rain."* For **Concept $C_3$**, the human rater highlights the Positive Evidence, *"the impact that temperature variations have on altitude contribute to the formation of rain."* Parts of answers corresponding to one piece of Evidence (positive or negative) do not need to be in the same sentence and could be scattered over a few lines.

Similar to the KE approach, we split the double-concept-based scored dataset into DEV and XVAL sets. However, the splitting is done according to the presence (or absence) of a concept. We use stratified sampling (Tucker, 1998) trying to uniformly split data such that each concept is represented in the DEV as well as the XVAL datasets. As mentioned earlier, the KE approach can include negative concepts; currently we do not use Negative Evidence automatically. In the remainder of this paper, Evidence is taken to mean the collection of Positive Evidence.

### 5.2 Automatically Selecting Model Sentences

**Motivation**

During manual MB with Alchemist, a model builder is guided by the complete set of students' answers in the DEV dataset, including holistic scores. Concept-based scoring allows a model builder, if we were to continue the manual MB, to be guided by concept-based scores and students' answers highlighted with the Evidence that corresponds to each concept when writing model sentences as shown, where $MS_{ij}$ entails $C_i$ and $E_{ir}$ entails $C_i$.

| *Concept* $C_i$ | *Evidence* $E_{ir}$ | $MS_{ij}$ |
|---|---|---|
| $C_1$ | $E_{11}$ | $MS_{11}$ |
| | $E_{1s1}$ | $MS_{1t1}$ |
| $C_2$ | $E_{21}$ | $MS_{21}$ |
| | $E_{2s2}$ | $MS_{2t2}$ |
| $C_n$ | ... | ... |

Further, students may misspell, write ungrammatically, or use incomplete sentences. Hence, Evidence may contain spelling and grammatical errors. Evidence may also be in the form of incomplete sentences. Although human model builders generating sentences with Alchemist are asked to write complete $MS_{ij}$, there is no reason why $MS_{ij}$ needs to be in the form of complete sentences. The NLP tools in the c-rater engine can cope with a reasonable amount of misspelled words as well as ungrammatical and/or incomplete sentences.

We observe the following:

1. Concepts are seen as a set of model sentences that are subsumed by the list of model sentences built by humans
2. Evidence is seen as a list of model "sentences" that nearly subsume the set generated by humans (i.e., the intersection is not empty)

**Approach**

In the automatic approach, we select the Evidence highlighted in the DEV dataset as $MS_{ij}$s. We either choose the intersection of Evidence (i.e., where both human raters agree) or the union (i.e., highlighted by either human) as entailing a concept.

### 5.3 Automatically Selecting Required Lexicon

**Motivation**

Required lexicon for an item includes the most essential lexicon for this item. In the KE approach, the required lexicon is selected by the model builder, who makes a judgment about it. In Alchemist, a model builder is presented with a tokenized model sentence and s/he clicks on a token to select it as a required lexical entity.

We have observed that selecting required lexicon $RL_{ijk}$ involves ignoring or removing noise, such as stop-words (e.g., "a," "the," "to," etc.), from the presented model sentence. For example, a model builder may select the words, *"how," "rain," "formation,"* and *"winter"* in the model sentence *"How does rain formation occur in the winter?"* and ignore the rest. In addition, there might be words other than stop-words that can be ignored. For example, if a model builder writes, *"It may help Alice and scientists to know **how rain formation** occurs in the **winter**"* – the tokens *"scientists"* and *"Alice"* are not stop-words and can be ignored.

**Approach**

We evaluate five methods of automatically selecting the required lexicon:

1. Consider all tokens in $MS_{ij}$
2. Consider all tokens in $MS_{ij}$ without stop-words
3. Consider all heads of NPs and VPs (nouns and verbs)
4. Consider all heads of all various syntactic roles including adjectives and adverbs
5. Consider the lexicon with the highest mutual information measures, with all lexical tokens in model sentences corresponding to the same concept

The first method does not need any elaboration. In the following, we briefly elaborate on each of the other methods.

### 5.3.1 All Words Without Stop Lexicon

In addition to the list of stop-words provided in Van Rijsbergen's book (Rijsbergen, 2004) and the ones we extracted from WordNet 2.0 http://wordnet.princeton.edu/
(except for "zero," "minus," "plus," and "opposite"), we have developed a list of approximately 2,000 stop-words based on students' data. This includes various interjections and common short message service (SMS) abbreviations that are found in students' data (see Table 1 for examples).

| | | |
|---|---|---|
| 1. Umm | 2. Aka | 3. Coz |
| 4. Viz. | 5. e.g. | 6. Hmm |
| 7. Phew | 8. Aha | 9. Wow |
| 10. Ta | 11.Yippee | 12. NTHING |
| 13. Dont know | 14. Nada | 15. Guess |
| 16. Yoink | 17. RUOK | 18. SPK |

**Table 1**. Student-driven stop-words

### 5.3.2 Head Words of Noun and Verb Phrases

The feature extractor in c-rater, mentioned in Section 2, labels the various noun and verb phrases with a corresponding syntactic or semantic role using in-house developed rules. We extract the heads of these by simply considering the rightmost lexical entity with an expected POS tag, i.e., for noun phrases we look for the rightmost nominal lexical entity, for verb phrases we look for the rightmost verbs.

### 5.3.3 Head Words of all Phrases

We consider all phrases or syntactic roles, i.e., not only noun and verb phrases but also adjective and adverb phrases.

### 5.3.4 Words with Highest Mutual Information

The mutual information (MI) method measures the mutual dependence of two variables. MI in natural language tasks has been used for information retrieval (Manning et. al., 2008) and for feature selection in classification tasks (Stoyanchev and Stent, 2009).

Here, MI selects words that are indicative of the correct answer while filtering out the words that are also frequent in incorrect answers. Our algorithm selects a lexical term if it has high mutual dependence with a *correct concept* or Evidence in students' answers. For each term mentioned in a students' answer we compute mutual information measure (*I*):

$$I = \frac{N_{11}}{N} * log_2 \frac{N * N_{11}}{N_{1.} * N_{.1}} + \frac{N_{01}}{N} * log_2 \frac{N * N_{01}}{N_{0.} * N_{.1}} + \frac{N_{10}}{N} * log_2 \frac{N * N_{10}}{N_{1.} * N_{.0}} + \frac{N_{00}}{N} * log_2 \frac{N * N_{00}}{N_{0.} * N_{.0}}$$

where $N_{11}$ is the number of student answers with the term co-occurring with a correct concept or Evidence, $N_{01}$ is the number of student answers with a *correct concept* but without the term, $N_{10}$ is the number of student answers with the term but without a *correct concept*, $N_{00}$ is the number of student answers with neither the term nor a correct concept, $N_{1.}$ is the total number of student answers with the term, $N_{.1}$ is the total number of utterances with a *correct concept*, and *N* is the total number of utterances. The MI method selects the terms or words predictive of both presence and absence of a concept. In this task we are interested in finding the terms that indicate presence of a *correct concept*. We ignore the words that are more likely to occur without the concept (the words for which $N_{11} < N_{10}$). In this study, after looking at the list of words produced, we simply selected the top 40 words with the highest mutual information measure.

## 5.4 Automatically Selecting Similar Lexicon

**Motivation**

In the KE approach, once a model builder selects a required word, a screen on Alchemist lists similar words extracted automatically from Dekang Lin's dependency-based thesaurus. The model builder can also use other resources like Roget's thesaurus (http://gutenberg.org/etext/22) and WordNet 3.0 (http://wordnet.princeton.edu/). The model builder can also write her/his own words that s/he believes are similar to the required word.

**Approach**

Other than choosing no similar lexicon to a required word *W*, automatically selecting similar lexicon consists of the following experiments:

1. All words similar to *W* in Dekang Lin's generated list
2. Direct synonyms for *W* or its lemma from WordNet 3.0 (excluding compounds). Compounds are excluded because we noticed many irrelevant compounds that could not replace uni-grams in our data.
3. All similar words for *W* or its lemma from WordNet 3.0, i.e., direct synonyms, related words and hypernyms (excluding compounds). Hypernyms of *W* are restricted to a maximum of 2 levels up from *W*

To summarize, for each concept in the KE approach, a model builder writes a set of Model Sentences, manually selects Required Lexicon and Similar Lexicon for each required word. In the automated approach, all of the above is selected automatically. Table 2 summarizes the methods or experiments. We refer to a method or experiment in the order of selection of $RL_{ijk}$ and $SL_{ijkt}$; e.g., we denote the method where all words were required and similar lexicon chosen from WordNet Direct synonyms by AWD. HSVocWA denotes the method where heads of NPs and VPs with similar words from WordNet All, i.e., direct, related, and hypernyms are selected. A method name preceded by I or U refers to Evidence Intersection or Union, respectively. For each item, there are 40 experiments/methods performed with Evidence as model sentences.

| Model Sentences | Required Lexicon | Similar Lexicon |
|---|---|---|
| Concepts (**C**) | All words (**A**) | None chosen (**N**) |
| Evidence Intersection (**I**) | All words with no stop-words (**S**) | Lin all (**L**) |
| Evidence Union (**U**) | Heads of NPs and VPs (**HSvoc**)<br>Heads of all phrases (**HA**) | WordNet direct synonyms (**WD**)<br>WordNet all similar words (**WA**) |
| | Highest Mutual information measure (**M**) | |

**Table 2.** Parameters and "Values" of Model Building

Before presenting the evaluation results, we make a note about spelling correction. c-rater has its own automatic spelling corrector. Here, we only outline how spelling correction relates to a model. In the KE approach, model sentences are assumed to not having spelling errors. We use the model sentences, the stimulus (if it exists), and the prompt of the item for additional guidance to select the correctly-spelled word from a list of potential correctly-spelled words designated by the spelling corrector. On the other hand, the Evidence can be misspelled. Consequently, when the Evidence is considered for model sentences, the spelling corrector first performs spelling correction on the Evidence, using stimulus, concepts, and prompts as guides. The students' answers are then corrected, as in the KE approach.

## 6 Evaluation

The study involves 12 test items developed at ETS for grades 7 and 8. There are seven Reading Comprehension items, denoted R1-R7 and five Mathematics items, denoted M1-M5. Score points for the items range from 0 to 3 and the number of concepts ranges from 2 to 7. The answers for these items were collected in schools in Maine, USA. The number of answers collected for each item ranges from 190-264. Answers were concept-based scored by two human raters (H1, H2). We split the double-scored students' answers available into DEV (90-100 answers), XVAL (40-50) and BLIND (60-114). Training data refer to DEV together with XVAL datasets. Results are reported in terms of un-weighted kappa, representing scoring agreement with humans on the BLIND dataset. H1/2 refers to the agreement between the two humans, c-H1/2 denotes the average of kappa values between c-rater and each human (c-H1 and c-H2). Table 3 reports the best kappa over the 40 experiments on BLIND (Auto I or U). The baseline (Auto C) uses concepts as model sentences.

| Item | #Training (Blind) | H1/2 | Manual | Auto C | Auto I or U |
|---|---|---|---|---|---|
| | | | c-H1/2 | c-H1/2 | c-H1/2 |
| **R1** | 150 (114) | 1.0 | **0.94** | 0.51 | **0.97** |
| **R2** | 150 (113) | 0.76 | **0.69** | 0.28 | **0.76** |
| **R3** | 150 (107) | 0.96 | **0.87** | 0.18 | **0.88** |
| **R4** | 150 (66) | 0.77 | **0.71** | 0.46 | **0.75** |
| **R5** | 130 (60) | 0.71 | **0.58** | 0.22 | **0.61** |
| **R6** | 130 (61) | 0.71 | **0.73** | 0.23 | **0.77** |
| **R7** | 130 (61) | 0.87 | **0.55** | 0.42 | **0.42** |
| **M1** | 130 (67) | 0.71 | **0.6** | 0.0 | **0.66** |
| **M2** | 130 (67) | 0.8 | **0.71** | 0.54 | **0.67** |
| **M3** | 130 (67) | 0.86 | **0.76** | 0.0 | **0.79** |
| **M4** | 130 (67) | 0.87 | **0.82** | 0.13 | **0.82** |
| **M5** | 130 (67) | 0.77 | **0.63** | 0.29 | **0.65** |

**Table 3.** Best on BLIND over all experiments

The accuracy using the automated approach with Evidence as model sentences is comparable to that of the KE approach (noted in the column labeled, "Manual") with a 0.1 maximum difference in un-weighted kappa statistics. The first methods (in terms of running order) yielding the best results for the items (in order of appearance in Table 3) are ISWD, ISW, ISN, IMN, IHSVocN, UHALA, ISN, UHSVocN, SLA, ISN, IHAN and IHSVocWA. The methods yielding the best results (regardless of running order) for all items using the Evidence were:

| | | |
|---|---|---|
| IHAN | U/IHAWD | IHAWA |
| U/IHALA | U/IHSvocN | IHSvocWA |
| UHSvocLA | UHSvocWA | UHSvocWD |
| U/ISLA | U/ISN | U/ISWA |
| U/ISWD | U/IAWA | IMN |
| IMWD | | |

This approach was only evaluated on a small number of items. We expect that some methods will outperform others through additional evaluation.

In an operational setting (i.e., not a research environment), we must choose a model before we score the BLIND data. Hence, a voting strategy over all the experiments has to be devised based on the results on DEV and XVAL. Following our original logic, i.e., using XVAL to avoid over-fitting and predicting the results of BLIND, we implemented a simple voting strategy. We considered c-H1/2 on XVAL for each experiment. We found the maximum over all the c-H1/2 for all experiments. The model corresponding to the maximum was considered the model for the item and used to score the BLIND data. When there was a tie, the first method to yield the maximum *W* chosen. Table 4 shows the results on BLIND using the voting strategy. The results are comparable to those of the manual approach except for R7 which has 7 concepts, the highest number of concepts among all items. The results also show that the voting strategy did not select the "best" model or experiment. We notice that some methods were better in detecting whether an answer entailed a concept *C* than detecting whether it entailed another concept *D*, specified for the same item. This implies that the voting strategy will have to be a function that not only considers the overall kappa agreement (i.e., holistic scores), but concept-based agreement (i.e., using concept-based scores). Next, we noticed that for R7, XVAL did not predict the results on BLIND. This was mainly due to the inability to apply stratified sampling with such a small sample size when there are 7 concepts involved. Further, we may need to take advantage of the training data differently, e.g. an *n*-fold cross-validation approach. Finally, when there is a tie, factors other than running order should be considered.

| Item | #Training (Blind) | H1/2 | Manual | Auto (C) | Auto (I or U) |
|---|---|---|---|---|---|
| | | | c-H1/2 | c-H1/2 | c-H1/2 |
| **R1** | 150 (114) | 1.0 | **0.94** | 0.51 | **0.88** |
| **R2** | 150 (113) | 0.76 | **0.69** | 0.18 | **0.61** |
| **R3** | 150 (107) | 0.96 | **0.87** | 0.18 | **0.86** |
| **R4** | 150 (66) | 0.77 | **0.71** | 0.38 | **0.67** |
| **R5** | 130 (60) | 0.71 | **0.58** | 0.17 | **0.51** |
| **R6** | 130 (61) | 0.71 | **0.73** | 0.13 | **0.73** |
| **R7** | 130 (61) | 0.87 | **0.55** | 0.39 | **0.16** |
| **M1** | 130 67) | 0.71 | **0.6** | 0.0 | **0.65** |
| **M2** | 130 67) | 0.8 | **0.71** | 0.54 | **0.58** |
| **M3** | 130 67) | 0.86 | **0.76** | 0.0 | **0.79** |
| **M4** | 130 67) | 0.87 | **0.82** | 0.13 | **0.68** |
| **M5** | 130 67) | 0.77 | **0.63** | 0.26 | **0.49** |

**Table 4**. Voting Strategy results on BLIND

In all of the above experiments, the Evidence was corrected using the c-rater's automatic spelling corrector using the stimulus (in case of Reading), the concepts, and the prompts to guide the selection of the correctly-spelled words.

## 7 Conclusion

Analytic-based content scoring is an application of textual entailment. The complexity of the problem increases due to the noise in student data, the context of an item, and different subject areas. In this paper, we have shown that building a c-rater scoring model for an item can be reduced from 12 to 0 hours of human intervention with comparable scoring performance. This is a significant improvement on research to date using supervised techniques. In addition, as far as we know, no one other than Calvo et al. (2005) made any comparisons between a manually-built "thesaurus" (e.g. WordNet) and an automatically-generated "thesaurus" (e.g. Dekang Lin's database) in an NLP task or application prior to our work. Our next step is to evaluate (and refine) the approach on a larger set of items. Further improvements will include using Negative Evidence, automating concept-based scoring, investigating a context-sensitive selection of similar words using the students' answers and experimenting with various voting strategies. Finally, we need to compare the results reported using unsupervised techniques on the same items and datasets if possible.

## Acknowledgments

Special thanks to Michael Flor, Rene Lawless, Sarah Ohls and Waverely VanWinkle.

## References

Calvo H., Gelbukh A., and Kilgarriff A. (2005). Distributional thesaurus vs. WordNet: A comparison of backoff techniques for unsupervised PP attachment. In *CICLing*.

Christie, J.R. (1999). Automated essay marking for both content and style. In Proceedings of the 3rd International Computer Assisted Assessment Conference. Loughborough University. Loughborough, Uk.

Foltz, P.W. and Laham, D. and Landauer, T.K. (2003) Automated essay scoring. Applications to Educational technology. http://www-psych.nmsu.edu/%7Epfoltz/reprints/Edmedia99.html

Leacock, C. and Chodorow, M. (2003) C-rater: Automated Scoring of Short-Answer Questions. Computers and Humanities. pp. 389-405

Manning C. D., Raghavan P., and Sch¨utze H. (2008). Introduction to Information Retrieval. Cambridge University Press.

Mitchell, T. and Russel, T. and Broomhead, P. and Aldrige, N. (2002) Towards robust computerised marking of free-text responses. Proceedings of the 6th International Computer Assisted Assessment Conference.

Mohler M. and Mihalcea R (2009). Text-to-text Semantic Similarity for Automatic Short Answer Grading. Proceedings of the European Chapter of the Association for Computational Linguistics, Athens, Greece, March 2009.

Rosé, C. P. and Roque, A. and Bhembe, D. and VanLehn, K.. (2003) A hybrid text classification approach for analysis of student essays. Proceedings of the HLT-NAACL 03 Workshop on Educational Applications of NLP.

Stoyanchev S. and Stent A. (2009). Predicting Concept Types in User Corrections in Dialog. Proceedings of EACL Workshop on the Semantic Representation of Spoken Language. Athens, Greece.

Sukkarieh, J. Z., and Blackmore, J. (2009). c-rater: Automatic Content Scoring for Short Constructed Responses. Proceedings of the 22nd International Conference for the Florida Artificial Intelligence Research Society, Florida, USA.

Sukkarieh, J.Z. and Stephen G. Pulman (2005). Information Extraction and Machine Learning: Auto-marking short free-text responses for Science questions. Proceedings of the 12th International conference on Artificial Intelligence in Education, Amsterdam, The Netherlands.

Sukkarieh, J.Z. Pulman S. G. and Raikes, N. (2004). Auto-marking 2: An update on the UCLES-Oxford University research into using computational linguistics to score short, free text responses. Proceedings of the AIEA, Philadelphia, USA.

Sukkarieh, J. Z. and Pulman, S. G. and Raikes, N. (2003) Auto-marking: using computational linguistics to score short, free text responses. Proceedings of international association of educational assessment. *Manchester, UK.*

Tucker H. G. (1998) Mathematical Methods in Sample Surveys. Series on multivariate analysis Vol. 3. University of California, Irvine.

Van Rijsbergen C. J. ( 2004) The Geometry of Information Retrieval. Cambridge University Press. The Edinburgh Building, Cambridge, CB2 2RU, UK.

Vantage. (2000) A study of expert scoring and IntelliMetric scoring accuracy for dimensional scoring of grade 11 student writing responses. Technical report RB-397, Vantage Learning Tech.

# Presupposed Content and Entailments in Natural Language Inference

**David Clausen**
Department of Linguistics
Stanford University
clausend@stanford.edu

**Christopher D. Manning**
Departments of Computer Science and Linguistics
Stanford University
manning@cs.stanford.edu

## Abstract

Previous work has presented an accurate *natural logic* model for natural language inference. Other work has demonstrated the effectiveness of computing presuppositions for solving natural language inference problems. We extend this work to create a system for correctly computing lexical presuppositions and their interactions within the *natural logic* framework. The combination allows our system to properly handle presupposition projection from the lexical to the sentential level while taking advantage of the accuracy and coverage of the *natural logic* system. To solve an inference problem, our system computes a sequence of edits from premise to hypothesis. For each edit the system computes an entailment relation and a presupposition entailment relation. The relations are then separately composed according to a syntactic tree and the semantic properties of its nodes. Presuppositions are projected based on the properties of their syntactic and semantic environment. The edits are then composed and the resulting entailment relations are combined with the presupposition relation to yield an answer to the inference problem.

## 1 Introduction

Various approaches to the task of Natural Language Inference (NLI) have demonstrated distinct areas of expertise. Systems based on full semantic interpretation in first order logic are highly accurate but lack broad coverage, requiring large amounts of background knowledge to do open-domain NLI (Bos and Markert, 2006). Other systems based on statistical classifiers and machine learning achieve broad coverage but sacrifice accuracy by using shallow semantic representations (MacCartney et al., 2006). Natural logic was developed as a compromise between these two extremes (MacCartney and Manning, 2009). It makes use of rich semantic features while using syntactic representations closely related to the natural language surface strings to achieve broad coverage. Other work has demonstrated the effectiveness of lexically triggered inferences and presuppositions to the task of natural language entailment and contradiction detection (Nairn et al, 2006; Hickl et al., 2006).

The natural logic model attempted to integrate these insights but recognized the difficulty of treating presuppositions within their current framework. Natural logic models negation, monotonicity, lexical relations and implicatures together as part of a sentence's asserted content allowing them to be treated through a single projection mechanism. Presuppositions notoriously do not interact with these features although they do interact with other semantic features requiring a separate projection mechanism. We present a model for presupposition detection and computation separate from asserted content. We extend the natural logic model to compute lexically triggered presuppositions covered by Nairn et al. We then integrate this information to produce improved coverage for the NLI task.

## 2 Presuppositions

Presuppositions are propositions that are taken to be true as a prerequisite for uttering a sentence. The set of phenomena often grouped as presuppositions are diverse, although they are frequently systematically related to certain lexical items in a sentence, in which case they are said to be lexically triggered. Lexically triggered presuppositions like (1c) from (1a) can be used by an NLI system to expand the information available for solving a particular problem without full semantic interpretation.

(1a) Bush knew that Gore won the election.
(1b) Bush did not know that Gore won the election.
(1c) Gore won the election.
(1d) If Gore won the election, Bush knew that Gore won the election.

In (1a) the factive verb 'knew' triggers the local factive presupposition that the sentential complement 'Gore won the election' is true. (1a) is a simple sentence so the sentence as a whole



*Proceedings of the 2009 Workshop on Applied Textual Inference, ACL-IJCNLP 2009*, pages 70–73,
Suntec, Singapore, 6 August 2009. 

presupposes (1c) and we can make use of this information for an NLI problem. A defining feature of presuppositions is their invariance under negation so we have (1b) also entailing (1c). The factive presupposition is said to project through negation to become a presupposition of the entire sentence. In other cases such as the consequent of a conditional, the presupposition sometimes does not project so sentence (1d) does not presuppose (1c). Whether or not a lexically triggered local presupposition becomes a presupposition of the entire sentence is known as the problem of presupposition projection.

A complete treatment of the projection problem for all types of presupposition triggers is outside the bounds of current NLI systems but for most purposes we can compute presupposition projections based on a simple model first outlined by Karttunen (1973). The model categorizes lexical items as either filters, plugs or holes and uses these properties to determine how local presuppositions project upwards through a syntactic tree to become presuppositions of the entire sentence. Lexical items are categorized according to their effect on presuppositions they dominate syntactically. The verb 'realize' is a hole, and projects the presuppositions of its complement unchanged so (2a) has a sentential presupposition of (2c). The verb 'pretend' is a plug and projects none of the presuppositions of its complement so (2b) does not entail (2c). The conditional is a filter and will sometimes project the presuppositions of its antecedent and consequent based on the entailment relation that holds between the two. In the case of (1d) the antecedent entails the presupposition of the consequent so the presupposition of the consequent is not projected and it does not entail (1c).

(2a) Rehnquist realized Bush knew that Gore won the election
(2b) Rehnquist pretended Bush knew that Gore won the election
(2c) Gore won the election

The verbs 'realize' and 'pretend' represent two modest size classes of verbs and nouns called factives and antifactives. The sentential presuppositions for any given factive or antifactive operator depend on its position in the sentence's syntactic tree and the number and type of holes, plugs or filters that dominate it.

To implement this theory we model the local factivity presuppositions triggered by various sentential complement taking operators. We then calculate the presuppositions of the entire sentence by projecting the local presuppositions according to Karttunen's theory. For each operator our system traverses the sentence's syntactic tree from operator node to root calculating how the local factivity presuppositions project through the various holes, plugs and filters. The result is a set of sentential level presuppositions that can be used to determine inference relations to other sentences.

## 3 Presupposition in NatLog

The NatLog system of MacCartney and Manning (2008; 2009) is a multi-stage NLI system that decomposes the NLI task into 5 stages: (1) linguistic analysis, (2) alignment, (3) lexical entailment classification, (4) entailment projection, and (5) entailment composition. The NatLog architecture and the theory of presupposition projection outlined in section 2 reflect two parallel methods for computing entailment relations between premise and hypothesis. We augment the NatLog system at steps (1), (4) and (5) to compute entailment relations and presuppositions in parallel. The result is two separate entailment relations which are combined to form an answer to an NLI problem. At stage (1) we calculate the lexically triggered factivity presuppositions for a given sentence. At stage (4) we project the presuppositions to determine the effective factivity according to the theory outlined in section 2. In stage (5) we compose the presuppositions across the alignment between premise and hypothesis to determine the presupposition entailment relation. Finally we combine the presupposition entailment relation with the entailment relation generated from the standard NatLog system to produce a more informed inference.

### 3.1 Lexical Factivity Presuppositions

Lexical factivity presuppositions are detected by regular expressions over lemmatized lexical items taken from the classes of factive and antifactive verbs and nouns. Figure 1 gives example entries for two operators. A sentence is analyzed for factivity operators by matching the regular expressions to the tree structure and when one is detected its terminal projection is marked as a factive operator with the appropriate factivity. The sentential complement of the operator is marked as being in the scope of a factive operator of the appropriate type.

```
Operator: know
Pattern: VP<(/^VB/</^know$/)
Scope: /^SBAR|S$/
Factivity: FACT

Operator: pretend
Pattern:
VP<(/^VB/</^pretend$/)
Scope: /^SBAR|S$/
Factivity: ANTI
```

Figure 1: A factive and antifactive operator

### 3.2 Presupposition Projection

For any given constituent of a sentence we can calculate its effective factivity presupposition by determining the number and type of factivity operators which dominate it. This is analogous to computing the projected presuppositions for a sentence but instead stores the information locally on the representation of the sentence. Let's compute the factivity of 'Gore won the election' in (2b). First we look for the immediately dominating factivity operator and find that it is dominated by the factive operator 'know' which assigns the local factivity FACT. We then traverse up the tree and find the operator 'pretend', which assigns the local factivity ANTI and dominates the constituent and the operator 'know'. We then compose the two according to table 1. to determine the effective factivity for the constituent is ANTI. If the sentence included more factive or antifactive operators we would continue to calculate the effective factivity recursively using the effective factivity output at each level as the dominated input for the next level.

| Dominated | Dominating | Effective |
|---|---|---|
| ANTI | ANTI | ANTI |
| ANTI | FACT | ANTI |
| FACT | ANTI | ANTI |
| FACT | FACT | FACT |

Table 1: The effective factivity for any pair of dominated and dominating factivity assignments.

The result tells us that the sentence in (2b) has an antifactive presupposition that 'Gore won the election'. This is equivalent to the presupposition that 'Gore did not win the election'. This contradicts (2c) and we can conclude that (2b) does not entail (2c). Detecting that the presuppositions of a premise are incompatible with the hypothesis is achieved in step (5) presupposition composition.

### 3.3 Presupposition Composition

The NatLog model for NLI computes a sequence of atomic edits from premise to hypothesis. The entailment relation between each atomic edit is computed and then composed across the sequence of edits to determine the entailment relation that holds between premise and hypothesis. An atomic edit consists of an insertion (INS), deletion (DELN) or substitution (SUB) operation. To compose the presuppositions calculated in step (4) we compare the factivity presuppositions before and after each atomic edit. In our simplified model the only edits that can change the factivity presuppositions are INS, DELN or SUB of factive or antifactive operators. Using table 2 we compute an atomic presupposition entailment relation between each atomic edit based on the edit type, local factivity and effective factivity. We then compose the atomic presupposition entailment relations to produce the presupposition entailment relation that holds between the premise and the conclusion. Finally we combine the presupposition entailment relation with the entailment relation generated by the standard NatLog architecture to yield the answer to the NLI problem. Atomic presuppositions are computed according to table 2.

| Operator | DEL | INS |
|---|---|---|
| ANTI | Alternation | Alternation |
| FACT | Forward | Reverse |

Table 2: Operator effective factivity and the resulting atomic presupposition entailment relation for DEL and INS edits.

The sequence of atomic edits converting the premise (2b) to the hypothesis (2c) involves DEL of one antifactive operator 'pretend' and one factive operator 'know'. The first DEL of 'pretend' results in an atomic presupposition entailment relation of Alternation. The second DEL of 'know' results in an atomic presupposition entailment relation of Forward, together yielding a presupposition entailment relation between the premise and hypothesis of Alternation. This allows our system to correctly predict (2c) is incompatible with and a contradiction of (2b).

## 4 Improvements

Previous implementations of the NatLog system were unable to handle NLI problems with (1b) as the premise and (1c) as the hypothesis because atomic presupposition entailment relations were treated together with normal entailment relations. The sequence of atomic edits from (1b) to (1c) would involve the DEL of 'know' resulting in an atomic entailment relation of Forward while DEL of 'not' would result in an atomic entailment relation of Negation together yielding Alternation instead of Forward. Our augmented system handles these types of inferences by separating presupposition entailment relations from normal entailment relations. In our augmented system only the DEL edit of 'know' produces an atomic presupposition entailment relation of Forward. Since no other operators in (1b) produce atomic presupposition entailment relations the resulting presupposition entailment relation between (1b) and (1c) is the correct Forward entailment.

Evaluating on a set of 3-way entailment NLI test problems developed at PARC by the authors of (Nairn et al. 2006) the Augmented NatLog system achieved an accuracy of 60.53% compared to the original NatLog system accuracy of 53.95% by correctly treating problems like (3) where (3b) should be inferred form (3a).

(3a) Bush didn't realize that Afghanistan is landlocked.
(3b) Afghanistan is landlocked.

With further development we expect to extend these results to other NLI test sets.

## 5 Conclusion

Our system extends the coverage of the NatLog system to correctly handle factive presuppositions. By computing entailments based on semantic containment and exclusion separately from those based on presupposition we avoid unwanted interaction between the two dimensions of meaning while leveraging the information contained in presuppositions to improve NLI performance. Although they are invariant under negation, presuppositions do not uniformly project. Projection is determined by a myriad of complex factors which ultimately require logical formalisms much more complex than predicate logic to compute (Beaver 2001). Our treatment does not currently take into account other types of presuppositions including those based on aspectual relations, (Mary has/hasn't stopped beating her boyfriend ⇒ Mary has been beating her boyfriend), definitine descriptions, (The king of France is/isn't bald ⇒ There is a king of France), or iteratives, (The boy cried/didn't cry wolf again ⇒ The boy cried wolf before). We have, however, provided a framework that can be extended to compute many types of lexically triggered presupposition and their projections. This work continues the theme of MacCartney and Manning in asserting "open-domain NLI is likely to require combining disparate reasoners". By augmenting NatLog with a reasoner based on factive presuppositions we take one step closer to the goal of achieving open-domain NLI.

## References


Beaver, David I. 2001. *Presupposition and assertion in dynamic semantics.* Stanford: CSLI.

Bos, Johan and Katja Markert. 2006. When logical inference helps determining textual entailment (and when it doesn't). In *Proceedings of the Second PASCAL Challenges Workshop on Recognizing Textual Entailment.*

Hickl, Andrew, John Williams, Jeremy Bensley, Kirk Roberts, Bryan Rink, and Ying Shi. 2006. Recognizing textual entailment with LCC's GROUNDHOG system. In *Proceedings of the Second PASCAL Challenges Workshop on Recognizing Textual Entailment.*

Karttunen, Lauri. 1973. Presuppositions of compound sentences. *Linguistic Inquiry* 4: 169-93.

MacCartney Bill, Trond Grenager, Marie-Catherine de Marneffe, Daniel Cer, and Christopher D. Manning. 2006. Learning to recognize features of valid textual entailments. In *Proceedings of the North American Association of Computational Linguistics (NAACL-06).*

MacCartney, Bill and Christopher D. Manning. 2007. Natural logic for textual inference. In *ACL-07 Workshop on Textual Entailment and Paraphrasing*, Prague.

MacCartney, Bill and Christopher D. Manning. 2008. Modeling semantic containment and exclusion in natural language inference. In *Proceedings of Coling-08.*

MacCartney, Bill and Christopher D. Manning. 2009. An extended model of natural logic. In *The Eight International Conference on Computational Semantics (IWCS-8)*, Tilburg, Netherlands, January 2009

Nairn, Rowan, Cleo Condoravdi, and Lauri Karttunen. 2006. Computing relative polarity for textual inference. In *Proceedings of ICoS-5 (Inference in Computational Semantics)*, Buxton, UK.

# Author Index

**Association for Computational Linguistics**
209 N. Eighth Street
Stroudsburg, Pennsylvania 18360